From the Inside Out

Also edited by Morty Diamond
Trans/Love:
Radical Sex, Love & Relationships Beyond the Gender Binary

From the Inside Out

Radical Gender Transformation, FTM and Beyond

Edited by

Morty Diamond

Manic D Press
San Francisco

Cover design: Scott Idleman/BLINK

Library of Congress Cataloging-in-Publication Data

From the inside out : radical gender transformation, FTM and beyond / edited by Morty Diamond.
    p. cm.
  ISBN 0-916397-96-3 (trade pbk. original : alk. paper)
  1. Transsexuals' writings, American. 2. Transsexuals—Literary collections. 3. Transsexualism—Literary collections. 4. Gender identity—Literary collections. 5. American literature—21st century. I. Diamond, Morty, 1975-
  PS508.T73F76 2004
  810.8'092066—dc22
                                            2004018230

CONTENTS

Breaking the Gender Mold

When I began compiling material for this book, I was going through a very emotional stage of my life. My transition began in late 1999 and for the next year I rediscovered myself as a transgendered person. Unlike many friends who began their transitions by taking testosterone, I waited a full year before taking hormones. By postponing hormone therapy I allowed myself time to develop my own thoughts about gender roles, and where I felt I stood. When I started the hormones I was just beginning to feel a sense of pride and certainty about being a gender variant person.

As a writer, I was eager to find books that reflected my views and could help me to understand other people's experiences about their own gender explorations. I was not looking for a clinical examination of gender deviation, but rather firsthand stories representing an assortment of voices and viewpoints. To my disappointment, many books discussed transgender people in a rigid structure of female-to-male or male-to-female. This system of classification overlooked other ways in which people choose to express gender. I was taking testosterone, but never wanted to become a man. Rather, I wished to become a gender that was neither male nor female. Living in San Francisco, I was fortunate to be able to meet others in the community who wished to remain outside of the binary world of male or female. These people, along with my own feelings about being trans, reinforced my belief that our experiences deserve recognition by the LGBT and straight communities.

More importantly, I wished to create a book in which the experiences of female-to-male (FTM) transgender men could be read alongside the stories of those who also started their life as female, but identify as something else entirely. Although we all identify and express our gender differently, our struggle for this freedom is the same. This book focuses specifically on those of us who were assigned female at birth, but who do not identify as female fully or at all.

Finding contributors for this anthology was an exciting experience. To my great delight there were many gender variant persons who were willing to share their stories. I also discovered the many ways in which people transition. This diversity in experience added to the many ways the contributors identify themselves: gender variant, transgender, third gender, non-gender, monster trans, mtm, genderqueer, transman, trannyboy, ftm, transsexual. Despite these differences in self-identification, background, and lifestyle, we all share a common bond of determining for ourselves what it means to live as a gender variant person.

These writers allow us a firsthand look into their own experiences with the complexities of sex and gender. From Michael Hernandez writing about sex and disclosure to Dean Spade giving us his story about pronoun usage, each of these stories gives the reader insight into how we live, and who we are. I found the poetry of Rian Fierros and Mac McCord to be very powerful words about their lives, and how they have unfolded. One of the more important aspects of this book is that it contains writing from an entire range of backgrounds including race, class, and sexual orientation. My deepest appreciation goes to all of the writers, whose work made this book a reality.

I would also like to thank to a few people without whom this book would not exist: Mattilda Bernstein Sycamore, Blake Nemec, Lee Krist, Chelsea Starr … you have all inspired me and helped me in so many countless ways. Special thanks goes to Rhani Remedes: you are a constant in a world of inconsistencies. To Kris Alexanderson, thank you endlessly for being so amazing, I'm the luckiest tranny in the world to have you in my life. To all the trans pioneers that have helped pave the way for the rest of us, thanking you is not enough, we owe our lives to you. Books like this have the ability to inspire more of us to live free, join the struggle, and eradicate the repression that surrounds our lives.

It is essential that more work shed light on gender freedom in the world. I urge others to speak up, contribute, write books, paint, film, organize, talk back, and come together to dissolve the written and unwritten rules. We must continue to keep the dialogue open if we are to achieve a place in the world where gender is allowed to be expressed by an individual however they please. To all who have ever said, "This doesn't work for me," and stepped out of the clutches of what society deems right; your liberation is meaningful to us all.

Morty Diamond
New York, NY

Transgressive Lust
Michael M. Hernandez

Lust is about passion. About desire. About satisfaction. Lust, for me, is an intense feeling most easily triggered by smell, materializing in the pit of my belly. The smell of a new leather jacket; the pungency and muskiness of sweat exuded during fear or intense excitement; sandalwood, sage, or a particular cologne. Smell alone can be enough to set me off. It's a purely chemical reaction to stimuli, fraught with an almost obsessive desire to taste, smell and feed the intense craving that usually manifests when I least expect it.

May 1997. I've bellied up to the bar and I'm waiting for the overworked bartender to bring back the overpriced domestic beer and Jack Daniels/Coke that I ordered ten minutes ago. It's hot. The number of bodies jammed into the room serves to choke out any measurable benefit provided by the air conditioning unit that I suspect actually works under normal circumstances. But these aren't normal circumstances, as evidenced by the overwhelming aroma of testosterone and sweat blended perfectly with the unmistakable scent of leather and Crisco. Perhaps the Crisco is simply my imagination running wild. These pungent blends of fragrance are starting to make my head swim and serve to trigger a variety of memories. In my mind's eye I catch short glimpses of images such as piss scenes, the sounds of fucking in the stairwells, cigars, a dance where you could cut through the feelings of lust and raw sensuality with a knife. I saw things through different eyes then and different eyes saw me.

I am brought out of my reverie by an odd sensation of being watched. Out of the corner of my eye I spy a hot-looking man staring at me. He has *that look* on his face and a huge grin to boot.

Anyone who has seen "that look" can tell you when it happens. It's sort of a cross between the wantonness of *I'd-jump-ya-if-I-had-half-the-chance* and the coyness of *I'm-a-shy-kinda-guy*. It has taken me quite some time to realize that I could be on the receiving end of that type of look. I have a knack for being clueless when someone is sending those telltale nonverbal signals of attraction. That's because I'm short, stocky, overwhelmingly furry, bald or balding depending on your perspective and have a tendency to channel intensity, often forgetting to smile. It is the intensity and lack of outward friendliness that has often served to discourage any potential tricks/fuckbuddies from approaching me.

Through time I have learned that what I am is bear bait. Despite this new understanding of attraction and flirtation, new encounters can prove difficult. I don't do terribly well with subtle hints. I tend to be blunt about what I want and prefer bluntness in return. "I wanna _____" works quite nicely when directed at me, thank you very much, but this direct approach seems not to be in vogue.

The guy eyeballing me is in no hurry. I've got a live one, but I'm not here to fuck. Well, I am, but I'm not. Sex for me requires some preliminary groundwork of the talking variety. Sometimes it works out and other times it does not. I have learned to enjoy the sexual tension, that delicious ache throbbing in the pit of my belly, the boiling of my blood, the stirring of my loins.

My drinks finally arrived. I gather them and make my way back out to join my party. Several minutes later, he's headed my way and I'm more than a little tense. Cruising is fun, but I am relatively certain that it isn't going to go any further than that. Once the cat is out of the bag "thanks, but no thanks" is often the reply. This may seem negative on my part, but in actuality my pessimism has served to reduce the tension associated with first encounters. In a perverse way, this is going to be fun. He sits down next to me. Conversation doesn't exactly cease, but I can tell that my friends are gearing up to practice the fine arts of voyeurism.

"Good evening, Sir." *Mmm, manners too.*

"Hi," I reply, flashing my best grin. We make some idle chit-chat and it doesn't take long before he starts to play with my arm hair. *Oh, this is going to get interesting.*

"Oh, I'm sorry, I should have asked for permission first," he says coyly. He knows exactly what he's doing and so do I. All of a sudden it's hotter than I remembered it being in the room a few minutes ago. My forehead has broken out into a sweat and I feel a stirring south of the equator.

"That feels good," I reply. "I'm very flattered, but I'm not what you're looking for."

"Yes, you are, Sir." Such a sweet boy. I know better. This is old territory for me, but more than likely new territory for him. In a short time, we are going to have that discussion which will potentially fuck everything up. THE conversation. You know the one. It's part of the price paid for my transgressions and my lust in all of its wondrous variation. Life is going to get a hell of a lot more complicated in just a few seconds. I carefully lock gazes with him trying not to look too intense and take a deep breath . . . here goes everything . . err . . .nothing.

I realize that I am holding my breath and have broken out in a sweat, two things that I have honed into a fine art. My odd habit of zeroing in on certain peculiarities while missing the obvious is off and running. His eyebrows are what first captured my attention. Dark, wild, and waxed at an angle that could be equally sinister or playful, depending on your point of view and clearly related to his mood. There was something about him that I couldn't quite put my finger on, but the flames of desire were certainly stirred. It was this mystery that drew me in. That and the fact that his eyes twinkled mischievously. This is the greatest attraction for me. There is so much information and emotion conveyed through these orbs, so often ignored in our porn and our lives.

He has dark hair, light eyes, and a full bushy beard. Fortunately for me, the attraction appeared to be mutual, but the timing was bad. He and his lover were just getting over the flu. My old man and I were getting ready to leave town in the morning. We chatted ever so briefly, but I knew where to find him.

The next time I came into town I made certain to look him up. I was all geared up for the chat this time. As fate would have it we wound up at the same party, small enough to be intimate, but large enough to make it interesting. We flirted with our eyes for most of the night, then at the end of the party he hugs me from behind and puts his hand down my shirt, playing with my nipples. I get hard just thinking about this. He had what can be described as a nice touch, just the right amount of pressure bordering on pain, and just enough gentleness to bring the full essence of pleasure through. I, being radio-controlled by these two nubs of flesh, was squirming. I could feel the heat radiating from his groin as his hard-on poked me in the back. At least now he has this little bit of information, but can I be sure that he *understands*? If there weren't so many other people in the room, I would have thrown him on the floor and started in right there. Well, maybe it wasn't just the presence of other people.

Exercising the greatest restraint, we take our appointed places and play out our respective mystery roles. It's all I can do to concentrate. After the party ends it isn't long before this hot bear of a man is working his hand up one leg of my shorts and is honing in on my jock. So much for talking first. Talking, however, is looming on the immediate horizon.

Put yourself in the following position: Your eyes fall on someone that you are immediately attracted to. It's a random encounter. You know nothing about the stranger, but at the same time you felt your cock stir in your pants. What is it about *him* that attracted your attention? I know, I know, at the moment that's not what you were doing at all. No one I know spends a lot of, or any, time dissecting their desire in the moment. If they did, the object of that desire wouldn't be there when they were done with their analysis. He'd be busy interacting with someone else. Humor me for an instant. Think about it. What did you really know about the guy that got your dick hard? I would venture to say nothing at all. Is there anything that he could say that would change your mind about your attraction to him?

I've had *this* particular conversation more times than I can remember, but it never seems to get much easier. The level of difficulty depends on what kind of headspace I'm in. That, and the realization that "no" isn't really about me. Well, it is and it isn't. It's about him and the decisions that he has to make for himself about the risks of interacting with me on a sexual level. That and how my little revelation is going to change his perspective of what he wants or thought that he wanted. To what degree will the bomb I'm about to drop alter our respective realities? He will need to weigh and balance the longterm ramifications of our chance encounter(s). Yes, I am hoping that there will be more than one. I was never really good at one-night stands which leave me wishing that there had been more time to explore something or another.

We are in sexually charged space and I'm not willing to look a gift horse in the mouth. I insist that I'm probably not what he's looking for tonight. He tells me that he's noticed the red hankie in my left pocket and while he's not into fisting, he is sure that we can work something out. He may be eating his words in a few moments. Here comes that talk that I was mentioning. There's no turning back and I really have no way of knowing how he's going to react. Fortunately the recent issue of *Canadian Male*, which happens to be sitting on the coffee table, is going to make this just a wee bit easier.

"Mmm, have you heard about Loren Cameron's book?" I ask nonchalantly, hoping that he has.

"No," he replies.

"Well, take a quick look at this review." I wait patiently for him to scan the 250 words of text that perfectly sets the stage for what I want to talk to him about. I look closely at his face waiting to see a trace of surprise, disappointment, anger… anything that will give me a clue as to how to explain what I need to without ruining the moment for either one of us.

"That's okay, Sir, I understand."

Now I'm perplexed. Being the pessimist that I am, I am certain that I just misheard what he said. Kind of like the night I heard my partner say he was going to cook the cat when what he really said was that he was going to take out the trash. My ears play tricks on me sometimes. I am convinced that this is one of those times. He couldn't possible have agreed to let me bury my dick up his ass.

He must have seen the puzzlement on my face because he

says, "I have friends who like to cross-dress." A light goes off over my head. He still doesn't have the slightest clue. This guy thinks I'm a drag queen and he must think that I'm a horrible one at that. I'm covered in fur and lack the kind of talent that it takes to get all dolled up in those tight clothes and high heels.

"No, I'm transgendered."

"Really, it's okay. "

I shake my head and laugh to myself. Invisibility: is it my bane or my blessing? "No, you don't understand. How shall I put this? I wasn't born what society traditionally considers male."

Now it's his turn to be puzzled.

"Being transgendered is a two-way street."

He gets it now. The fact that his jaw has dropped is a significant indication of that. It also reveals the gist of what he's thinking. *If I'm gay, how could I have possibly been attracted to him . . . um . . . her. . .um . . . him. Whatever! Does this mean that I'm straight? Bi?*

When I said that we needed to chat he assumed that I was going to tell him that I was HIV positive. He now understands why I was so sure that he was looking for someone else. It's not that I'm selling myself short here. I'm sure that under the appropriate circumstances we could have negotiated something that would have been mutually enjoyable and safe to our respective psyches. Yet I knew that the amount of discussion usually needed to assure someone that their attraction to me does not alter their sexual orientation could not happen within the span of time available on this occasion. There are so many other options readily available this weekend and so little time. It would take several hours, if not years, to sort through these issues. That's because my story is relatively new.

The numbers of openly queer and gay identified transmen is increasing, but on the whole our invisibility remains intact. There is very little porn about us. We represent the unknown, and as such, have not yet been eroticized and/or fetishized. It is the unknown that makes us a little unsettling to another's sense of self. At the same time, we pique the interest. What do our bodies look like? How do we smell? Do we ejaculate? Do we like getting fucked, fucking or both? What is off limits and what isn't? Only the most adventurous or the most secure venture into these waters. The fact of the matter is that each of us is different. Generalizations don't work. No assumption would be a correct one to make.

You couldn't pick me out of a crowd or tell what I'm into by looking at me, but you might be pleasantly surprised by what you find. I have a full beard, am covered in hair except for my head, have talented hands, a wicked grin, an impish sense of humor, and pride in who I am. Yes, I do get hard-ons and can ejaculate if you hit just the right spot. No, I haven't had a dick surgically constructed, there are too many other things that I could do with $150,000. What I have was grown by better living through chemistry — testosterone. If you are looking for more than a mouthful, you have the wrong fella, but we could go for a wild ride with a strap-on.

I do fuck on the first date, but don't assume that you will be the one doing the fucking. Don't expect me to become overly attached, but expect a call from time to time or even e-mail. I thrive for the delicious ecstasy of feeling flesh on flesh, tasting sweat and latex, and inhaling all of those aromas that only serve to fan the flame of yearning.

In short, I'm looking for adventure with a man who has a sense of humor, an open mind, who is comfortable enough with his body that he knows what he likes and who's not afraid that I get his cock hard. Someone who loves having their nipples tweaked, twisted, pinched, sucked, caressed and tormented in general. The guy that gets hard just thinking about having his cock and balls slathered in Tiger Balm. Someone who sees me for who I am, a mischievous little imp in bear's clothing, searching for sexual nirvana. That delicate balance between agony (evidenced by squirming) and ecstasy (evidenced by moans) is what gets me off… That is where my lust resides.

Your gender doesn't matter, so long as you are intriguing. The packaging simply adds texture.

American Transsexual Sacrifice
Tucker Lieberman

Stranded! The hotel management thought they'd have been rid of us by now, the hundreds of teen punks who descended on their posh lobby, the dull roar of our conversation echoing in the glass atrium from sunrise to sunrise. We planned to leave on Sunday but we are stranded. The two feet of snow that arrived during the 2003 True Spirit conference shut down Washington, D.C. and none of us are going anywhere.

I look up at the ceiling of this hall where I will be stranded for some hours or days. Whoever designed the Washington Court hotel must have had a blast. The safety barriers on the mezzanine are made of glass so the room feels paradoxically open and closed, like a glimpse inside the womb at our own translucent fingers. The ceiling is adorned with glass pyramids, each with eight reinforcements that deliver a large swath of sky. Downstairs there is a maze of ballrooms, some of which are only accessible by crossing through others. Rooms inside rooms inside rooms. It was not claustrophobic or limiting. The more intricacies we realized, the more space there was.

There is room for me, the bread and butter of this conference, a classic transsexual who transitioned five years ago. I happen to be gay and my romantic interest in males (mostly theoretical) has never changed. I cannot compete for queer hipness with the sex-crazed poly-pan-sexual teens who somehow leave me feeling, at my long-haired 22 years of age, nearly like an establishment figure. But I keep coming to these conferences because I believe there is room for all of us.

By opening itself up to us, the hotel becomes larger. Every person miraculously finds a seat, a workshop, a neighbor. As if in Willy Wonka's Great Glass Elevator, we seem to crash through the glass pyramids that make up the third floor ceiling as we race ten stories higher.

Not everyone here looks familiar to my own heart. I've never lusted for a transboi or a woman, never desired cleavage or a smooth round belly, and I don't identify with people who do. As a gay man, I don't always feel much in common with lesbians, and as a romantic, I have more interest in marital pageants than with nightclub ruts. I come to transgender conferences knowing that my limited interest in sexuality and my stabilized gender identity could be a conversation killer. I have to figure out what it is I want to discuss, what it is I'm still doing here after five years of contented life in my chosen gender.

"Queer culture" is supposed to unify us, but truth be told, the word "queer" means very little to me. No one ever derogated me or other gay boys that way when I was growing up, nor did I ever feel that being gay or transsexual was unnatural. I've always felt that the people who never questioned their gender, sexuality, marriage, or fertility were the odd ones. If anyone needs an outsider's label, it's the ones who moralize against human sexuality, not the ones who accept it.

There were people at True Spirit who agreed with me: we're not minorities. "Who the hell is the majority?" asked keynote speaker Dr. Ibrahim Farajaje. What would a sexual minority look like? A thirteen-year-old who isn't interested in pornography? Everyone has desires and revulsions that come as part of their sexual configuration package. While we can organize ourselves into queer subgroups of microscopic scale, we also participate in the universal condition of human sexuality. There is nothing "minor" about consciously using sexuality as a tool in our personal liberation.

Nor am I fond of the term "non-traditional". My involvement in the gay and transgendered community is approaching eight years. We have many traditions—pride marches, potlucks, lobby days, choral groups, adoption agencies, sitcoms, dark alleys, commitment ceremonies, religious services—and who is to say they are not traditional simply because they are not heterosexual?

If not "queer," "sexual minority," or "non-traditional," I don't know what to call this group of people in the Washington Court Hotel. I know that our camaraderie is about our sexual differences. And yet, on another level, it isn't.

It is not about sex, that insanity that makes one's belly the center of the cosmos. Think bigger. That is, think of oneself as smaller, and the universe as hanging on a variety of other luminous beings besides one's own holy genitalia. As it started to snow in Washington, the glass elevator rose through a flurry over the thousand-strong crowd who lounged in the yellow indoor glow. A glass ceiling shielded them from the flakes. They appeared, from my perspective in the surging elevator, to be in a snowglobe, that quaint protector of timelessness and innocence. From a distance I could just make out the spiked purple hair, the beards, the range of body shapes, the boldly embracing dykes, and yet there was a sameness to every human being who lounged on the couches or scampered up the stairs. The sealed glass channel gave no hint of the clamor until it plunged down through the ceiling again and opened the doors in the lobby.

It is not about sex, that insanity that makes one's belly the center of the cosmos. There are other centers. The Washington Court, for example, was designed to be a center: a hotel for conventions where anyone can press a button and soar above their clan and see what a mass of transgenderism looks like from a distance. This city is a center: a few blocks away, the awesome dome of the US Capitol shines like the midnight sun. Decisions are forged, ideals are set, promises broken, history painted one leaf at a time. The sky is a center: on Sunday morning, the heavens glaze over and set adrift a calming, stiffening whiteness over cities and plains, incontrovertible proof that the natural elements still hold all the true power in this world. And there are a number of centers on every body: the deep-set eyes, the signing hands, the jewels, the secret spots of pain and of endearment. On all these things, on glaciers, on fingertips, on governments, on tribes, the universe is drawn.

We are at the True Spirit conference because we are sexual beings. But our sexuality is not what the sky is focused on, and ultimately, not even what we are focused on, whether we realize it or not. There are other callings, other directions we are pulled in, other meanings of being a soul.

The sheer number of people crowded into the hotel is overwhelming to me. On Saturday night, instead of going to the sexual "play party," I read Thomas Cahill's *The Gifts of the Jews*. He discusses the Biblical authors' realizations that God wants their spiritual inwardness, not their outward display of piety. Simple, but it struck home.

I think of myself as a channel. Energy passes through me,

converted and transformed. Tonight I feel like a birdhouse. The dead wood harboring fragile new life. Transition long past, I maintain the health of my transsexual body, gut it, prepare it to host whatever fertile spirits may lodge there beyond my control or knowledge.

The language of sacrifice in mythology has always been paradoxical, ripping us from logic as it rips us from our families. Like Abraham, we in the United States are preparing to sacrifice what we love. Even if this war truly is a defense of freedom, in our deliberate initiation of force we are simultaneously sacrificing some of our freedom. Freedom to live, for the soldiers. Freedom to be presumed peaceful, for the government. Freedom from fear, for the civilians. Freedom from the moral responsibility to rebuild a devastated nation. Freedom from blood on our hands. Freedom to mind our own business and pretend we live in simpler times.

The written word of the desert god says that we must fear him because he can kill us and yet not fear him because he is on our side. Our president says to fear terrorism from the desert because nerve agents can dissolve our brains and yet not to fear it because no one dares to mess with an angry Republican. I can think of another reason not to be afraid of terrorism: our willingness to sacrifice everything abolishes our fear of loss. Transgendered people know what sacrifice is. One of my MTF friends has spoken of transition as "crossing the fear barrier." We feel commanded to do this crazy thing, to slash the ropes of family ties and crush the bones of our previous values. As we start to walk through the fire, we have the opportunity for a reprieve, as Abraham also received: we do not have to be murderers and no one has to die. We can transition safely and usually less catastrophically than we feared. But by our willingness to have made the worst possible sacrifice, we are reborn and have a new relationship with the powers that be.

I close my eyes. I am in the shadow of the Capitol. I have taken a train to Washington on an "orange alert" weekend. I am offering myself up as a sacrifice which, if it were to happen during a sudden terrorist attack, would not be easy for the world to understand, clean up, and move past. I am the American transsexual sacrifice. Every transgendered person here is a self-sacrifice for world peace. We are counting on an angel to stay the hand of the slayer.

We are diplomats. We are go-betweens for men and women. This is true whether we embrace or deny it. We are here to make peace with ourselves, our lovers, other transgendered people, and to carve out a home in the cliffs that sprang up between the sexes. We belong to the holy order of the self sacrificing diplomats.

The snow falls faster. The glass ceiling has been dusted to opacity. When I am perched high above it, I can no longer see what lies beneath the veil, until the elevator falls all the way through it.

What is gender? The toys you collect, the length of your hair, the sport you play, the locker room you piss in, the parent you emulate, the sex you're attracted to, the position you assume with them? No, those are just signs, conventional markers of our gender identity. Maybe what gender is really about is learning to be a balanced, kind, independent person? No, even harmony, compassion, and liberty are just signs of the soul's greater freedom.

It doesn't matter that I'm not like the transdykes, the polyamorous, the straight FTMs, or the men and women at the conference who are attracted to us. Whatever gender current or gender vector we have, whether our birdhouse hollow points toward the rising or the setting sun or the harvest moon, we are all pursuing the question of how to be at peace with our bodies in the world and to realize, through that peace, the true meaning of it all. At that point, gender is no longer about navigating one's life between two categories. It no longer matters who is a gentle, gay, dickless transsexual exactly like me and who is "trans: other". Gender can be a way of discovering our deepest common human nature. Because when all the signs are stripped away, what's left is our pursuit of truth and peace.

John Rawls, an important twentieth-century philosopher who died last year, said that the road to social justice requires us to imagine a "veil of ignorance." If we could choose the sort of society we would be born into, but could not choose the particular body we were to inhabit, what society would we choose? An unequal social order would make it probable that we would be born into oppressed bodies. The veil of ignorance about the circumstances of one's birth, then, provides incentive for an unborn angel to engineer a society where everyone has a chance to pursue happiness. Once you lift the veil, it is too late. You have to plan for the future. And what you assume to be other people's future could in fact be your future.

The elevator tears through the snow-coated roof into the honey-colored lobby. The moment of parturition has arrived. I will be one of the bodies in this room, although I am not sure which one. That is not my direct concern. My task is to make a good life for myself by making a good life for all. Five years post-transition, it comes to that.

I do not understand the dykes, the former dykes, the street punks, the straight men, the promiscuous, the trannylovers, the breasted, the cocked, the shamed, the shameless. I do not have to understand them. Our similarity is our revelation that we are processing the mystery of everything under the sun through the common lens of transgenderism. Our eyes lock onto one another, probe, and, humbly, greet each other. Good morning.

The Conversation
Cooper Lee Bombardier

I.

Is it your tits? Why don't you just get your tits cut off and be a dyke? You always were my lumberjack guy. I just think it's more radical to walk the line in between. I like the contradiction between your gender and your body. You know I love you, Cooper, but I don't know why you'd want to be a man – I just don't like men!

All butches are gender dysphoric!

What's wrong with being butch? What's wrong with being a dyke? Why would you want to cut up your body like that? You are the perfect man for me, Cooper Lee. I don't understand what makes you so different from all the butches I've slept with. I think you are the butchest person I've ever slept with. You are a real man. Are we third sex, Cooper? I am just afraid you won't want to do dyke things anymore. Don't be afraid to confront the boss – you are more of a man than he is! It's just your internalized misogyny. I am afraid we won't be read as queer anymore, I mean, I am a dyke! I like butches who are into their tits! All of the butches are becoming men – who am I going to date now? I just think that if you can find some way to be happy in the body you have, you should try to do that. It just seems like a really hard life to be transsexual. If that is what you decide to do, I can go through that with you.

Someone asked me if I had a big brother named Cooper in San Francisco. I said, "Hell, yeah!"

Do you prefer "He" or "She"?

I will love you no matter what.

II.

Before I knew I was a human being and not a dog, my earliest sense of myself was male. I am just a funny sort of guy. I don't hate my female body; I just don't recognize it as mine. I wouldn't trade the path of my life for anything. I am glad I was raised female. I don't even like to take Advil. I don't like the idea of needing the permission of a doctor or shrink to get what I want. Haven't they invented "Boobs-Away" cream yet? It isn't about "becoming" another person – I already am who I am – I just want my body to reflect that. It's not like I am suddenly changing from the person you've always known – this is more about your willingness to see who I've always been.

You don't have to understand – you just have to believe me.

I didn't know the dyke nation could be so easily shaken. I am afraid of losing my community. I've done a lot for this community – what difference does it make how I identify? I think it's far more radical to proudly say who you are and be vocal about it than to be invisible out of fear of rejection. It's not my responsibility to keep the world of dykes sacrosanct.

This would kill my parents. I wonder if I'll get fired.

I am not sure which is worse: feeling invisible as a tranny when being perceived as a butch dyke or feeling invisible as a queer when being perceived as a man. There is nothing wrong with being butch, except for the fact that I don't feel like a woman. I have never been a woman having sex with another woman.

I wish people got as excited about all of the differences between each other as much as they get excited about all the different kinds of dogs in the park.

No, I'm the boyfriend.

I'm your man. I'm the porridge Goldilocks picked – just *right*.

"He" just feels more true.

I think of myself as this dude but around the guys at work I realize I am not one of them, either.

I am happy with my cock the way it is.

Nobody passes in San Francisco.

Everyday we each must learn again how to love ourselves. I wonder what it feels like to be at home in your body. It's nice of you to promise to stay but people hardly ever do. I have been on the outside my whole life, I am not afraid of being outside.

I don't want to disappear into the world as a straight man.

I don't want to disappear into the world.

I don't want to disappear.

Some Kind of Queer
Jordy Jones

Why do you listen to that faggot music? I was seething,
breathing deeply. My cousin was all boy. Real boy. I was quick on
the ball. What are you, some kind of queer? Yeah. Some kind. It
was 1982 in Tucson, Arizona. I looked across the breakfast table
at the boy-cousin. I had been sent here to go to high school. It
wasn't my doing, but it was only temporary. I dreamed of escape.
No pain, no joy, no power too great, a chance to die, to turn to
mold. Listening to the music on the headphones. I said, "Do it
again, do it again." My aunt looked worried. She was a little bit
afraid of me 'cause love won't make me cry. I had cold fire. Like
to take a cement fix. I was the Prince. I had read Machiavelli. And
Shakespeare, and Plato, and Marx. I was fifteen.

Changes. I ran across a monster sleeping by a tree, and I
looked and frowned and the monster was me. I had seen Harvey
Milk on television. Harvey died but he saved my life. In walked
luck and you looked in time. And David Bowie saved my life.
Feeling so gay, feeling gay. Yeah, some kind of queer. A lifetime
of brothers, sons and grandsons had driven my aunt to decorate

poodles. She tried to decorate me. Transition. Transmission. Oblivious to her disappointment, I equipped myself with a glam-boy wardrobe of flare-leg jeans and shiny shirts with big collars. You wanna be there when they count up the dudes. Dressed like a priest you was. Tod Browning's freak you was. I locked myself in my room and listened to Bowie on headphones: a girl who looked like a boy who liked boys and didn't even have the decency to be good at sports. When you're a boy other boys check you out. Wonder who, wonder who, wonder when. On another floor, in the back of a car. If you want it, boys, get it here, thing. Be a standing cinema. Some kind of queer. I took my boyfriend up to the balcony at Frank Lloyd Wright's Gammage Auditorium at ASU to fuck. He was awful nice... really quite out of sight. I stood spread-legged holding the railing, looking into the night sky, waiting for the space invader.

Hold on to nothing, and he won't let you down. Life stands still and stares. Ziggy came out of a dorm-room somewhere. My knees were shaking, my cheeks aflame. Drive me there, darling. Taking it hard, taking it hard. Nothing will corrupt us nothing will compete; thank God heaven left us standing on our feet. I came blinking beyond the horizon, and he came in my ass with his eyes shut tight. Life is a pop of the cherry. We're fighting with the eyes of the blind. Hard wet and innocent before the plague. If his trade is a curse, then I'll bless you. Holy, holy. Some kind of queer.

Monster Trans
Boots Potential

As a kid, I had a fascination with monsters. I'd check books out of the library full of movie stills from *Dracula*, *The Werewolf*, *Frankenstein*, *King Kong*, and *The Swamp Monster*. The monsters and mutants always scared me shitless and inspired nightmares of all flavors. But I kept going back for more of the same. As any adrenaline junkie kid will tell you, the sheer heart-pumping, palm-sweating terror is the best part. The intrigue with monsters gradually waned as I entered late grade school, preferring to acculturate myself to the *Pretty in Pink*s and *Breakfast Club*s of the time. However, like any healthy obsession, it gradually worked its way back into action. I began to appreciate the *Friday the 13th* and *Nightmare on Elm Street* slasher flicks (taking a short break for a terribly sincere and plaintive boycott since my feminist consciousness dictated I avoid such maliciously misogynistic garbage). And along with my burgeoning affection for punk rock, zines, and other pleasantries, I developed an infatuation with B-movie classics. By way of the Misfits, I learned titles to various Ed Wood, Jr. greats: *Astro-Zombies*, *Plan 9 From Outer Space*, and *Night of the Ghouls*. In my junior high-age, nerdy juvenile delinquency (and only half in jest), I identified with these mutant, misunderstood outcasts. I will never make claim to a coherent gender narrative.

I could tell you a story about my childhood that would surely predict a queer adulthood: crushes on teenage girl camp counselors, tomboy androgyny and jock identity, Transformers and Tonka trucks, and stealing boys' Underoos from friends' dresser drawers. Similarly, and just as truthfully, I could order my childhood into a perfect predictor of heterosexual and gender-normative fulfillment: cute boyfriends who I thought were hot, a darling collection of stuffed animals and Pretty Ponies, and a subscription to *Seventeen* magazine. To this end, I will never say that my early fascination with monsters was all about my being a queer genderfreak transboygirl fagdyke. I will say, though, that there has always been something compelling to me about a living (or undead) thing that can freak the shit out of someone just by merit of their very existence in the world. Especially when, in doing so, it forces us to question the boundaries of the things we once thought were neat, well-defined, and impermeable (human, animal, inanimate object, living, dead, etc).

My preoccupation with monsters has mutated into something that provides me with an index with which to enact my gender and transness. Cultivating my monster identity preceded my identifying as trans. Part of the reason for this is the rule-breaking nature of monstrosity. For awhile, I was swindled into thinking, as many of us are, that there is a "correct" way to be trans: we have to take hormones, get surgeries, get a GID diagnosis, change pronouns, pass, feel like a boy in a girl's body, and get a preppy haircut. My inclination is to break rules or flee from them, and if this long list of rigorous requirements was what it took to be trans, I didn't want that.

It was clear to me that I was involved in some sort of gender subversion project. For a long time, my queerness has been in large part about widening possibilities of gender expression. I didn't (and still don't) buy the story that there is something fundamentally dichotomous about gender, and that there are inherent or genetic characteristics that lead to expressions of femininity or masculinity (whatever those terms mean). Unfortunately, being in queer communities didn't necessarily mean that people agreed with me on that point. In fact, many homos that I know are quite wedded to conventional understandings of gender and its rules of conduct. When I became frustrated with all of these "play-by-the-rules" queers, I sought out freakier communities. Some did drag and some put on rock operas about animal-human creatures that subvert the futuristic corporate stranglehold on the world. With these people, I found a number of things I was looking for: political engagement, creativity, an unquenchable urge to fuck shit up, and most importantly, a passion for boundary transgression and rule-breaking. In and through my work and play with these communities (conversations, drag acts, writings, and so on), my fascination with monsters moved from spectatorship to embodiment. I became the monsters I used to watch.

The monster identity, however, is an imperfect model. I do not necessarily want to associate myself with viciousness, irrational violence, and pathological insanity (although mainstream culture has already associated these with queers and trannies, so perhaps it's not so far a stretch). Nevertheless, there is something very promising about a monster culture that might revel in itself, that might deliberately position itself as monstrous in the sense that it deviates, threatens, and challenges. As in the case of gender freaks (i.e., trans, genderqueer, FTM, MTF, multigendered, and so on), it is only the common experience of transgression that defines monsters and arranges them together as a group. Frankenstein,

Vampira, and the Creature from the Black Lagoon have nothing in common but their "abnormalities", yet they are bound by their monstrosity. This is how I make sense of my gender. It is defined largely by what it isn't (normative). However, it is also defined by what this disruption of "normal" opens up.

Monsters are often referred to as "it." Though "it" is not my pronoun of choice, I am heartened by the thought that a living thing (at least within the collective imagination of a filmic audience) can escape immediate relegation to one category of the sexual dichotomy or the other. Like many genderqueers and freaky trannies, I perceive a profound lack of options when it comes to pronouns. "She" fits no better than "he." For a time, I continued to use "she" in part to disrupt the notion of what a trans person is allowed to be and partly in resistance to adopting the other end of an "either/or" choice. At this point, more to articulate my gender incoherence than to find a pronoun that "fits" or "feels right", I usually use male pronouns or the pronoun "monster." Many medical, GLBTQ, and trans communities would often have us think there is no other way than to choose consistent male or female pronouns, or there is something wrong with us, with our transness, or both. Monsters, on the other hand, open up a wealth of possibilities: what do you call someone or something that eludes you to the point that you can't determine its species or origin, let alone gender?

Monsters demand this of people in their very existence. Their rule-breaking bodies and actions necessitate a navigation of language that is unfamiliar and uncomfortable to a normative audience. This is what I would like both my gender and my pronoun to do: create the necessity to navigate language and the concept of gender in a way that is unfamiliar and demands thought and critical engagement. Similarly, monsters open up new and unfamiliar categories with regard to their bodies. They often fall outside of the set of prescriptions that define female- or male-bodied people. It is often useless to attempt to determine their "kind" (whether animal, plant, person, or thing) because they are rarely a member of an easily defined "kind." They may be a hybrid (werewolf, swamp monster), an undead human (vampire, zombie), a semi-human/machine (Frankenstein, Astro-Zombie), and so on. All of these are frightening partly because they defy their kind. They are never entirely what they are supposed to be, and we are able to read this transgression on their bodies. I plan to seek surgical alteration of my gendered chest. I am not intending to "pass," my goal is rather to be able to be read as trans, to create a lack of gender-cohesiveness on my body. In other words, I aim to defy the "kind" that I am supposed to be, true to my monstrous affiliations.

We queers often make the mistake of replicating the conventions we initially intend to defy. How often have we heard proponents of gay marriage or gays in the military talk about liberation? How often have our sexual practices and identities been policed by other queers (e.g., dykes and fags can't sleep together; femmes can't be FTMs; butches can't fuck butches; trannies should always try to pass; MTFs have to hate penetrating during sex; etc.)? It seems that we queers in particular have a lot to learn about the monstrous habit of staking out new ground and in doing away with, rather than duplicating, the rules.

The drawbacks of associating with monstrosity are rather clear. Monsters are associated with evil, bloodthirsty violence, and aggression. Monsters populate nightmares and haunted houses. They are beings, real or imaginary, to avoid at all costs (except when we watch them in movies or read about them in comics and books). Less obviously, but equally importantly, the concept of monsters has racial implications. Monsters are oftentimes associated in negative and damaging ways with "darkness" and "blackness". They are "foreign" in many different senses, lending to a sense of xenophobia. There is a none-too-subtle connection made between the "monster" and the "savage", a well-worn racist term historically used by colonizers and anthropologists to indict populations of people with cultural habits different from their own, and to justify attempts to colonize, enslave, or persecute them. These are the connotations of monstrosity that I wish to avoid, disrupt, and question.

Film and fiction cultures have a history of subtle and overt racism that often plays out in "monster" stories, and this is unacceptable. At the root of these problems is a deathly fear of difference. It is in and through this terror of those that appear foreign to us that we superimpose upon them a sense of danger. We make the monster by seeing it as scary. I think it is entirely possible to divorce the concept of "monster" from an inherent evil. Queers inspire fear in people because they fail to fit a prescribed social and societal norm of heterosexuality. So, too, in the case of monsters: they inspire fear not due to an inherent evil, but rather as a direct result of failing to conform to an expected set of standards as to what a living thing should be and look like. Furthermore, just as there are many varieties and embodiments of queerness, so too are there of monstrosity. However, it should be said that this strategic employment of monstrosity is at least partially enabled or at least made more accessible to me as a white person. It might look very different for a trans person of color to claim monstrosity as a gender identity. It should also be said that the multiple ways in which our bodies are classed, raced, gendered, abled, altered, made, and understood are in a constant and changing relationship with the ways in which these bodies are understood, policed, and interacted with daily. This means that the ways in which we claim any gender identity are culturally and socio-politically loaded along those matrices. This should not point to preclusion from forging or claiming various identities, but should encourage us to do so with a high degree of articulation and specificity.

My favorite monsters are the B-movie variety. This is the source from where my gender enactments are inspired. They manage to be at once deliberate in their freakishness, fictional, contrived, shocking, fascinating, never "correctly" human, always tenacious, and often campy. I take from this my pleasurable enactment and embodiment of transness. I revel in being freaky and campy, attempt to use the nervousness I inspire in people to challenge, and never settle into categories I don't feel accommodate me. And every once in awhile, just to punctuate my point, I wear an old-fashioned Martian mask for fun and for effect.

It is interesting that I came to identify as trans in and through my gender-as-monster ideas. There is more than just monster culture that preceded and inspired my identification as trans, and there is more to my transness than monstrosity. However, it is interesting how much easier it was to say, "I'm trans," when I had a tangible example and concept of how I could explain my transness outside of the medical model (of Gender Identity Disorder). For me, thinking about rule-breakers like B-movie monsters laid out a neat framework of what I want and expect out of transness. It makes anti-gender-cohesion as fun a game as it is a serious project. And of course, monstrosity and transness are both of those things.

The most hopeful and beautiful thing about monstrosity-as-gender is the fact that once you become a monster, nothing looks "normal." Everyone is a monster waiting to happen, they are just choosing, at the moment, to cohere to an arbitrary and fictional set of rules and regulations as to what they are supposed to be. You start inhabiting an entire world of monsters. And nothing looks better.

For a number of years, I have been aware that rule-transgression and other forms of productive and challenging delinquency are important projects to me in terms of gender and other personal and political questions. However, in the last few years of thinking about monstrosity and trans in relation to myself, the concrete ways in which I hope to enact those transgressions has become much less of a mystery. It is an answer that makes sense in reply to the question, "How can I approach gender in a way that is equal parts radical, fun, politically challenging, personally comfortable, and a serious and sustainable project?"

It suddenly feels like my project goals are dovetailing with the concrete ways I want to achieve those goals. I am thrilled to have a vehicle which allows me to be simultaneously politically engaged, campy as hell, tough-as-nails, sissy faggy, butch new-wave dykey, dead serious, boy-girl-whatever, pansy, and terrifying all in one fell swoop. Male/female dichotomies do not allow for this mobility and simultaneity, but monstrosity does. I find it extremely pleasurable that it is B-movie monsters that made it possible for me to pinpoint the way I want to do gender and the way I can make sense of my queerness and transness. For once, the story ends happily, and the monsters are the heroes.

A Trilogy of Horror and Transmutation
Ali Cannon

I. Frankenstein

If the creature emerged from rock
then now, two hormone injections later
I am transfused
like that Frankenstein movie scene
where the mad doctor is poised
as the lightning strikes
and the red punch dyed fluid
rushes through plastic tubing
and black and white studded extravaganza

Gene Wilder was poised and laughing
other doctors were more mad
but all were proud of their achievement
The monster lies waiting on the slab
dull and lifeless

at the moment of infusion
the bolt cracking

all the tissue igniting
the body raised from the dead

    when I get my first testosterone shot
    I'm lying like the creature on the slab
    my ass in the air awaiting that small stick
    which all my needlephobic anxieties rest upon

Jessica tells me sweet romantic highlights of our life together
        While I squeeze my FTM dad's hand
the injection is brief and after the nurse leaves I break down
        in the arms of my loved ones

it being a huge relief to have placed myself upon that slab
        the medical moment standing for so much
        in the scheme of monster making
but let's not forget

Frankenstein is gentle and fragile
even while prone to rages
that being a symptom of his abnormal brain
the tissue animated too quickly
or maybe just being too different and vulnerable
for the world he was thrust into

when I get my second shot I am joined by another FTM pal
        he gives me a headband with devil horns for strength
            I lie on the table with the devil on my side
            red stuffed velvet
            little horns sticking out
            above my head
        as I clutch his hand in my still present needlephobia
meanwhile the doctor stands over the creature
but the doctor is as much me as any medical professional

it being everyone's collective experiment
to deliver the transgendered unto themselves

        Frankenstein rises from the table
        one foot coming heavily to the ground
        a large echoing thud
        his movement is tentative
        and awkward

onlookers watch for signs of life
will he speak
or continue with his arms raised
that is the spectacle of it all
gentle reminder for the monster
so afraid to be walking at all
the lightning still flashes high in the sky
an archetypal conundrum

        Frankenstein ponders his maker
        the doctor still gleaming
        sure of his role
        but no creature is built

on someone else's notion of life alone
that is only the arrogant mad scientist's dream
which perhaps explains why many a monster
turns on his maker
as if to blame him for those mistakes

the slab is cold and hard
with the imprint of the once lifeless body
the cold granite holds him
to the shape of himself

it being neither lifeless
nor stony
but infused with the same ancient lightning
that now brings a broken smile
to the creature's tentative face

II. Creature from The Black Lagoon

transition, transgender
transmutation
mutation, permutation
the infinite possibilities of re-making
one's self
the possibilities of becoming
mutating into a different form
but not by gene
by hormone
I'm already mutating
a creepy oozing transformation
I'm oozing into my manhood
it's like the Creature
from the Black Lagoon
emerging from the ooze

>   the creature steps out
>   arching its clawed feet
>   onto the damp cement
>
>   no Grauman's Chinese Theatre
>   will mark its passing
>   no ice age will prepare its coming
>   it emerges out of the darkness

forested twilight
light barely reflected through
trees
sparks of dew
urging on a moist forming
of morning
morning like a raging fury
a cracked open
marble agate
rock encrusted
with layers of quartz
gray-green embers
sparkling within

the creature lived in that egg
for centuries
she pushed her granite toes out
into someone else's existence
she forged a human likeness of herself
no miners' hands could hold her back
she sprayed herself
with cool waters
from atop Rainbow Falls
that cracking open was hard work
her tail spat itself out
whipping around to brush away
a world of dissonance
scaled wonderment she thought
still longing for that cold, hard
rock egg
that was where she forged herself
alone in that wilderness
but not so cliché
her arching desire to become anew

this time was built upon
every monster movie ever made with compassion
the creature steps forward
onto gentle sands
wind whipping through her
tender eyelashes

passing through a fine mesh
so many dandelion puffs
cast along on air
he not prepared for the outrageous
fortune of it all
the cracked stone egg
lying like a remnant
on the volcanic edge of her soul
into this fire she leapt
she sang
she rocked herself silly
she waddled, she danced
she paraded around
it was all she could do to keep
from pushing her whole head
upwards through the roof
of her desire
that was what she wanted
emerging in this way
all the creatured parts of herself
and s/he
was not afraid
coming to this moment

III. The Wolf Man

Not only inspired by my recent facial hair growth
In the lexicon of horror archetypes
the Wolf Man is a being who changes
and then returns to a homeostatic state
a state of normalcy
without the mutating influences
but that is always there, always lurking under the surface
the more I live in the world of men
am seen as male
experience myself fully occupying this space

If assumed biological male
I wonder where and how I return
and to what state of previous normal
or previous anything
surrounded by bio men objectifying women to one another
through pornographic humor
in the stockroom of Nordstrom's Rack
caused me to feel less than comfortable with my mutated self
I felt returned to my secret woman's body
site of male violence
despite my hairy face
that doesn't give me away
how scary to imagine being found out
amidst this sacred territory
of men talking only with men
about women – the way I've always feared
knew it to be
how often this territory is demarcated by men
with and for one another
is probably not really known

by women
who are never there
to hear those without women conversations, gestures,
articulations
so there is this tension
a knowledge of myself
as one of them
and then not
the brotherhood extends its hands
and all the other intact body parts
Yesterday, two different gay men told me
how good I look
and that too is a sign of passing
but also a new venture
into a different predation
and that is certainly the guise of the Wolf Man
an unleashed predator
spun out of control
needing to feed
on any body
to satisfy its hunger
the bristling edges are not lost on me
as I walk anthropologically in this tranny path
my hairy self is just a beginning
of this entry where shadow selves
meet around the corner
and howling in agony
is only part of the unremembered dream
the next morning

Transsexual Fires
Patrick Skater

What would you think if your belly was full of fire, your nose choking with smoke rising from a rage so blinding you could not turn left or turn right but just stand staring out into a world you knew was enemy, no firemen in sight? How would you be nice then, appropriate, outstanding?

I stood under the lights of the ballfield and waited for my name to be called with the other boys so I could run out onto that grassy arena in my clean new uniform, run out there to play with the other guys, run out there through the cool evening air. But no one ever did call out my name, didn't call out. Didn't. And so I burned like so much after-game trash, in the back, under the stands, by the chipped tar, and my ashes formed into a mutant child.

I learned how to act nice, my mutant face smiling pleasantly. I learned how to appropriate, asking, "Would you like another cracker, Mrs. Eberhart?" My mutant eyes dull. I learned "outstanding" did not apply to mutants and then I tore the town apart, the windows breaking from my flames, combustion shattering the understanding of my parents' blank faces, no tears to end the destruction, no rain. Only shame. Theirs and mine. Our loneliness a blanket to roll in across the dirty floors of this enemy world.

What would you say if you could climb inside of me and know what fire burns there, where I have lived five hundred years in hiding? If you could feel the heat on my face each day I had to carry someone else's breasts on my firm and muscled chest?

You would suddenly say, "Oh God, I never had any idea…" and you would be sorry for the way you held the water back, your slippery fingers gripping the faucet, holding it tightly shut as you watched me consumed, my skeleton showing through as gristle and fat dripped down.

You would suddenly find yourself hysterical, you would, to know how dark you could be, like the crisp outer layer of barbecued chicken. How dead. You might even vomit to know, to feel for yourself the fire that made you laugh and whisper not so long ago.

I have forgiven you five thousand times. And hated you again five thousand more. I call myself freak when the pain gets to be too much. I scream it through the roar in my ears, through the red, the yellow, the orange that colors my every sight.

Sometimes I lay in my bed, over the covers, and rub my hands down my post-surgical body and I see only smoldering ruins, the birds cautiously chirping outside my window, the blaze died down, half-charred remains still identifiable around me. And I am delighted to imagine that perhaps I can rebuild after all. And I lean over and lift the shade oh so slowly to see if out there is forever enemy or if all these years I have missed something and in the quiet of my hiatus from hell there might be something more.

Winter (Transition)
Sailor Raven

This winter you are my lover. In the morning soft and new sometimes my hand slides past your bellybutton beyond the line where sometimes doctors look to find out what you are. Female. Male. A blurring of worlds, rules, the world's so-called rules. Between your legs my eyes and mouth speak, cruel. Every day your body changes, tidal. Our vision is transformative, navigating broken bodies like landscapes, recreating what's been spoiled. You are new in your own skin because I see you male, something else, something less simple. You are soft and harsh and raging. A photograph of your body with no face can be bewildering – this is not the boy I love. This is the particular fate passed down to you. Until two days ago the days were getting shorter, the darkness deeper. Now the transformations of light are in reverse.

You said last night that you're sorry, that you have this perfectly good body that you can't seem to really live in. I said, baby, it's not your fault. This is some sick trick played on you, bringing you out into the world in someone else's form and expecting you to find your own or live a trap for yourself all your life. A body owned and confined. The stunning comfort is that I find you within it. We go to sleep clinging to each other with goosebumps and a still-young anger. In the morning warm, my hands cupped firmly around your hipbones, nails scraping over ribcage, lips brushing your rough cheek, the tip of my tongue to your small cock. Sex is transformation as we bring each other into the bodies we thought we'd be, how we were meant to exist. The world's bright eyes glowing through the window onto us as the sun rises. Today there will be just a couple of extra minutes of light.

I pull your shirt up over your head. Slide my finger behind your belt. Slide my tongue below the waistline of your boxers. Suddenly naked you are a kind of male undefined, unrefined, stunning, your eyes sometimes wide with a fear of being otherwise. Through the din and mess of gender and sex, violation and ownership, I can see you, transparently watching yourself change. I find your body and know it piece by piece, both visible and invisible, create you in the morning as you wish to be born. We hurt and heal each other. You hold me tight sometimes, your head on my shoulder and thin arm across my waist. My hand on your bony back.

I can't begin to explain to you in weak words on paper what I feel of you, how I see you, see in you, which body of yours I adore. I adore the transformation, the fact of your indefiniteness. The physical collides with the mental, with our bodies of past lives and future realities, a divergence of the boys we were meant to be with the boys we are. They call it dysphoria but you are not that lost, you are everything at once. You are an infinite possibility with a body that I swim in some mornings with the first light, consumed. We are everything at once, touching without innocence, one moment violent, the next soft. As if drawing each other's blood. As if drawing each other's true bodies out on the sheets with damp fingers. Your body is tiny in my aching strong hands sometimes, making a small symphony of our strength together. The light through the window falls finally to illuminate your face, and as your eyes open your very skin changes. This morning I am your lover, your other body, a piece of a dynamic transition, a crescendo, a collapse. This morning you shiver with release as your voice grows deeper and your shoulder wide and strong. I scrape up against your skin your broken body healing as we collide. My broken skin merges into yours. Long shadows, a long story. You and I are easily transcendent between the sheets, as truth transforms anger in the pale ever-changing winter light.

Thoughts on Transcending Stone: The Tale of One Transgendered Man and His Journey to Find Sexuality in His New Skin
Marcus Rene Van

My search started outside of the bedroom. I've spent more than five years of studying and reconstructing myself as male. I studied men and how they move. The way their shoulders stay stiff and never sway when they turn: I did that, too. I watched the way inflated chests and arms filled invisible spaces. I learned their essence like a lost language. Now I am a master of embodiment. I am shifting, almost as if unzipping the outer shell of a female skin and stepping into *him*, who is crisp with clean-cut edges.

In the minds of some, this thing that I am — a man in a woman's skin — cannot exist. I've spent days intently watching the people around me, always wondering, "Am I passing for male? And if so, how long will it last until they know?" After this, it's hard to feel erotic and whole.

Sometimes the outside world can slip between my sheets like an unwanted menage á trois. The half-sneered "baby" from the man at the liquor store can castrate me instantly. Sometimes,

I can find my own stripped confirmation of self in the bedroom. It is a place to relax and let down the constant guard. The woes of the waning day slip away to memory.

In the bedroom I need a woman who sees the man I am, and treats me that way. It's difficult to be with a partner who is not understanding of transgender lovers. Even though I bring a strong sense of self-awareness to any sexual encounter, if a partner does not relate to me as male, it's hard to connect. I need a woman who can respect what I am.

My trans sexuality is the mental and physical pleasure existing in the same space. It's a fragile world, constructed on beliefs and acceptance, and mirrored in a partner's gaze. This is not to say that it is all a mind game: that undercuts the fact that the connection between partners is visceral and real. Our worlds are connected at some place that reaches beneath the surface. When she says, "You have a shaft," I believe her, and feel myself getting mini-hard on her fingers. Never mind that my dick is enclosed in the folded skin of labia.

I have always found sex fulfilling in a different way than most people. I was once fully stone: one who accepts little or no physical reciprocation. Sexual pleasure happened in my mind much more than my body. I refused to be completely naked during sex as not to expose the charade of maleness, my chest and dick were always shrouded in a cotton cocoon. My own fulfillment was something that rested solely on my partner's release. If she didn't come, then neither did I. When I encountered a partner who couldn't have an orgasm I understood that putting pressure on my partner's pleasure could be overwhelming.

Sometimes I feel that taking testosterone would make receiving physical reciprocation easier and less mental. I listen to many of my friends on testosterone tell stories of monstrous desires to be touched, and I admit, I get a little jealous. I think, *maybe testosterone is the catalyst.* I imagine them having unrestricted sexual interludes, postsurgical chests and engorged clits basking in unfathomable titillation. I once had a friend tell me that he was far more sexual in his maleness than he had ever been as a woman. At the time it was hard for me to understand because I was lost in a cycle of hating my own (female) body so much, I didn't see that there could be any way to love it.

Allowing myself to be unapologetically stone was crucial to my trans development. There was power in naming my desires and finding a way to be pleasantly sexual. However, I am not striving for a life that would make *Stone Butch Blues* look like a happy tale. Now I am finding ways to grow and exist in my body without losing my maleness. There *is* certain pretense – there has to be when the body and the mind have such different ideas of what I am. There is a way to combine the strength of physically passing for male in the outside world with who I am in bed. In the bedroom, I can drop the prefix. Trans trails off into just man. It becomes a second nature after a while. Basically now I feel like I'm a dude with a vagina but it is not a female part — it is simply a part of me as I always was and always will be. In fact, I should be the envy of biological men because I have one. What straight man wouldn't want to have a pussy with him at all times?

Lies
David Husted

I was told once by a friend that all transsexuals were terrible liars because their whole live they've had to lie about who they are. This seemed an odd statement at first but as I thought about it I realized she was probably right. I'm a terrible liar. I couldn't tell a fib if I had to and yet my whole life has been spent in the closet pretending to be 'normal'. I've lied about myself every day of my life—at least every day since kindergarten. I guess I'd have to say I was pretty successful at it, too. I think all transsexuals have to be good at it if they want to survive adolescence.

I was called the usual names, of course; after all, I was a tomboy so there were the all too common terms of 'dyke', 'queer', 'fag'. I never felt any of those were true. I wasn't a dyke or a lesbian — but was I butch? Oh yes. I was butch. I was so butch that I hid it behind long hair and Levi's. Oh, I'd be looked at as a holdover from the '60s, a late bloomer, a tomboy, anything except what I really was. For me, no word existed to say what I was, and that made me a freak. The F word. Nothing could be so cruel or so hard as that, and all my life I saw myself as just that, a freak, an indefinable thing. So now I know. There is a word for what I am. I am a transsexual. I am identifiable. I am a person. But how to tell the family? How do you tell someone that your life has been a lie? How to convince those who think they know you, that everything they believe is wrong?

Mom, you know how you always worried I was lesbian? Well, guess what? I'm a transsexual. Hey Dad, you remember that son you always wanted? Looks like I'm it after all. Well, bro, sis, I'm contemplating a sex change and I think we should sit down to discuss your feelings about it. It sounds so clinical, so easy, almost funny at times, but it's not. And that's the hardest step. Facing strangers isn't so bad. They're strangers after all, but facing your family is a whole other thing. Convincing them that this new, shocking, farfetched idea is something you've been dreaming about, wishing was possible. Having to deal with every single day of your life when all along they bought into the lies, the stereotyping, and the million and one things we all do to say, "I'm okay."

Well, — newsflash — I'm not okay. I need your love and your support. I need you to be happy for me that, for once in my life, I don't feel like the F word. For once, I feel whole. How can a parent or a sibling understand that? Maybe they can't and maybe they won't. Maybe it's why so many of us make our own families outside of familial bonds. Maybe it's why so many gays and lesbians, so many transgender people, have such close bonds in the families they create from their own subcultured worlds. We need that. We need to be touched and held. We need to cry and to be there for others to cry on. We need validation in our lives.

Closets kill. They suffocate us. We drown in the refuse of our own lies, the lies that say we're alright. We're only alright when we can be what we are and be seen for who we are. We're only alright when we're free to be ourselves, free of the lies, fears, and the rejection of those we need the most. Closets kill and coming out of closets can be terrifying and dangerous not just emotionally but physically as well. So what do I deal with? Trying to explain that this isn't new. That I've known for a long time who I am. Trying to convince those who have watched me grow up that I've tried hard to blend to cover up what I am, that I've been a liar all my life. Yes, I was butch, but no more than a million other girls who loved being girls. I didn't love it though. I hated it. How do you explain that the smiling face they know, the laughing, joking prankster was crying herself to sleep every night, was feeling such self-loathing, that it's hard to describe?

How do you make them understand that it was a cover? They won't believe it and they have a right not to. After all, that cover is a damn good one and people see what they want to see. No one wants to know what it feels like to feel that kind of anger, frustration, even self-hate. No one wants to think about it. Push it under the carpet and buy the lie of smiles. It's easy to do and it's not that hard to emulate. Sometimes there are only two ways to handle something: either break down and cry, or laugh. So we laugh and we cry only when we're alone and no one can see how really vulnerable we are. So I'm still butch. So I still only cry when I'm alone but I know I'm not alone anymore. I'm not unidentified. There are others like me, transmen, FTMs: men born in the wrong body and some of us are straight and some of us are gay but that doesn't really matter. What matters is that we're not alone and that no matter how long we've lived the lie — we don't have to die with it.

Will family members ever understand? Some will and some won't. Some have outright told me that I'll never be a man. "I just don't see it happening," one said. It's as if, for some of them, they think this is something new, something "cool". It's not. This is the biggest decision a person can make in his or her life, changing their sex is not something that happens overnight. It took years to build the lies up to make that cover solid and it will take time to break them down again. To let the truth come out, to act as myself without backing up into old habits of covering who I am.

The first step is to say, "I will not hide who I am any longer." And that is a huge step. It's the very first step in a long line of steps away from the lies and into the truth of self. I will not hide. I will be who I am. I will be who I was meant to be and I will not let others decide for me who I am. I'm the one who has to live in this body, not them. I'm the one who has to face my own reflection in that mirror every morning. Now I can face that reflection knowing I'm not alone, knowing that others have trod this same path. It's hard, but every small step forward is a victory. Crawling may be safe, it may be familiar and maybe we have to begin by crawling but we all learn to let go of the safety of confinement and we learn to walk upright. Fear isn't something that the brave never feel, it's something they feel very strongly and they face it anyway. Fear is letting go of the safety of the cover, the lie, and the shelter that is fabrication and saying, "This is who I am and I want to be seen for myself."

Pecos Bill
Rian Fierros

you were the man
I always looked up to
shoulders broad and strong
a wall of contradiction
stained with your tears
the ones no one
would ever see you cry
and hands like mine,
big and rough and right
for holding
holding me on your lap
holding me through my terror
of night
you never knew that
I would sneak into your closet
and pull out your old work shirts
and pants and boots
and play 'daddy'.
long enough

to feel the callus of your life
rubbing against me
the cement smell
of driveways and highways
stitched into the sweat
and blood soaked bones
of your hard labor
you never knew
that when you told me
you rode a twister
with Pecos Bill,
I believed you
and spent a long day
in the office of a man
who did not know you or me
trying to convince him
of this truth
the one you told me
my small ego beaten and defeated,
the punishment for my resistance.
you never knew that
when I played house
you were the husband
I wanted to be,
the man
I wanted to become.
I even took your name, Andrew.
you never knew that
it hurt me when you drank too much
and smelled like an ashtray
and hit mom
on more than one occasion.
I still hurt
when I remember the yelling

the screaming
the tension
of the predictable first hit.
when I got old enough,
I could fight back.
and I did.
tiptoeing in between the punches
meant for mom
on more than one
black-eyed,
bruised face,
swollen-assed, morning after
you would come into my room
and whisper to me as I slept
tears in your voice,
and shame
glistening off your cheeks…
at the foot of my bed,
you would sit
"mihija, I am sorry,"
you would whisper.
at ten years old,
I was able to forgive you
at ten years old
I was able to forget
because
you never knew that
while you sat at the foot of my bed
head bowing low and eyes closed
I was awake
and heard the pain
in your voice
shaking
felt the grip

of the fist of shame
as it tightened on your heart
and I
I could forgive you.
you worked hard
from the age of 14
to put food on the table for abuelita.
you were the father
to your 4 brothers
and your sister.
the one you named.
and when you turned 18,
you were daddy to me,
the first of twins,
and brandee 4 years later.
now some 15 years
of memories gone
and you cry yourself
to sleep
because
you have lost
your daughter,
your firstborn.
but I am here.
filled full of the strength
that made you proud
to call me your child
I am here.
still full of the words
that you taught me
I wish I could express
the depth of my love for you
I wish that when I said
you have the heart

and soul of the man
I most want to become
you would not cringe
at my words
I wish I could be your son.
could make you proud of me
the way you were proud
5 years ago
when I was small and pretty.

I wish that you
could have seen my
first steps into manhood
told me
what it would be like to shave.
what it would be like
to hold a woman in my arms
for the first time
as a man
but like you taught me
wishes don't come easy and
sometimes they come too late
if they come true at all
you never knew that
when I look in the mirror
I see your face
looking back at me
each day my form
takes the shape of you
this you do not know
but I am old enough
to walk this path alone and
without the help
of a man

who will not call me his son.
who will not call me
by the name I have chosen..
but the love that echoes between us
makes the days go by faster now.
and the nights,
the nights do not resist
the moon from shining.
you never knew that
on lonely days
I could see
out into the distance
out into the San Francisco sky
just above the fog
that rolls in
around this time
a man, my father
on the back of twister,
taming it.

Whose Masculinity Is It Anyway?
Wyatt Swindler

My two older brothers, who are 5 and 8 years older than me, have been my role models in every way. Especially in what it means to be a good person, as well as a masculine person. They were always sharing with me the evolution of their masculinity but I had never, until recently, really thought about my own in any concrete way.

In some ways I was socialized as both a boy and a girl. This has everything to do with where and when I grew up, and how I've presented myself. My parents gave up on making me act like a girl when I was 6 or 7. However, in many not so subtle ways, they treated me like a girl despite the ending of their outward attempts of feminization. I was always a girl to them, being more fragile or susceptible to harm. They thought I couldn't make intelligent decisions about my life. Some things were due to age, but most were not.

In the outside world, though, the predominantly straight-white-rich community that I was surrounded by saw me as a black boy. I had to deal with the fear, racism, and prejudice from these people. People who have learned that while it is not okay to say "nigger" in "mixed company," it is most appropriate to fear and hate young men like myself more than others. We are looked upon as criminals. Young black men manage to be both the epitome and the antithesis of masculinity: all that is feared and coveted of manhood. I have known these things since I was a young boy. In order to survive I've memorized the expectations and limitations of black masculinity. I have been hurt, silenced and terrorized by what it means to be a black man. After so many years of wanting to gain unqualified acceptance into the world of black men, I am realizing that I have much to learn about what it means for me to be one.

I have spent the past six months attempting to grow comfortable in my young-manhood but I have realized that I don't know how to express my masculinity in the outside world. Especially how to be myself around other men of color. I am afraid of being inauthentic. What does that mean? I am afraid of not being real (streetwise) or hard (not feminine), or masculine (straight) enough for other men, especially young men whose companionship I feel like I desperately need, to accept me as I am. What does that say about my ideas of masculinity then? It speaks more to my fears than anything but it also means I've been holding onto a lot of other people's ideas about what it means to be a man, especially a man of color.

I know what is acceptable once I leave the comfort of my genderqueer microcosm where self-identification takes precedence over body parts, voices, and names. I know that there are ways that I can act, ways that I can present myself when I step outside of my door so that people will not question who I am. It's hard not to fall into that. It's a battle I face everyday and it's a different battle depending on who, what, when and where.

I still have the hardest time around men of color. I want that community, but I too often feel that queerness is unacceptable, and then more and more things get piled onto the list of what men of color are not (that I, undoubtedly, am). So it begins that I have become yet another person limiting what other men can be against my will, against everything I have fought for my whole life. It is one of the hardest shackles to break, and it is part of my thoughts on everything from class, race, gender, and sexuality. Everything is fucked up in my head because of what I've either accepted, or too often striven to be more of a "real black man" to others and/or my completely overinvolved fears of not being seen for the young man I am.

When I was living in San Francisco and just beginning to live my life as a boy it was walking the streets of the Mission, Soma, and the Tenderloin that I would emerge alone, in the daytime. At night I was the kind of man I thought I had to be to be accepted. I would set my jaw, walk my brother's standard issue gangsta walk, look straight ahead and through anyone who might have even glanced at me. But it wasn't me, I am not a badass, I'm a tough kid when I need to be, but I'd rather never need to be. The front was annoying, all the back and forth began to scare me. I didn't want to turn myself into the version of my brothers that came out on the streets so I tried to tone it down. I tried to let myself be the same person alone in the outside world as I was with my friends. I was trying to find some sort of middle ground.

On my own, I tend to be seen as I wish to be seen on a much more regular basis. Older black men stop me on the street and tell me stories of their boyhood. Men nearer my age call me "young blood" or "little brother." I'm sure they assumed I was 15 or 16, which got on my nerves some days but mostly I took their words as the highest possible compliment, as acceptance into a world that I never thought I would find my way into.

Despite all my intentions of being myself, I have been

desperately afraid of other men thinking I was either a fag or acted like one (meaning NOT masculine, and therefore feminine, and possibly as not even a man). This fear goes against everything inside of me because I identify quite strongly as a fag and as a queer fag but I am sometimes afraid that if they thought me to be queer they would look harder and see what I have never been—a girl.

Many transguys devote a good deal of time trying to be taken correctly. Some have bought into what it means to be a Man as much as those socialized that way from birth. Some are trying incredibly hard to discover what masculinity and manhood mean for them. I've been denying the fact that my fears about not being accepted as a young man are based on social programming. My fears aren't invalid because of this. Most of the rest of residents of this country have been programmed along with me. My fears are many people's TRUTHS but I have to learn not to allow my fears to dictate the kind of person I am or the kind of person that others can be.

Often
Mac McCord

It isn't often that I sit and cry,
but I did today, after seeing
    a child at the store.
  He was about six, maybe seven, with short
    hair, wearing grubby jeans
      and a defiant expression.
  His face had tear streaks on dirty cheeks,
    and the mother looked embarrassed.
  She held a pair of pink sneakers in elegant hands,
    and walked steadfastly to the checkout
    counter. The child trailed behind her,
      staring at the floor.
"I wanted the shoes like Daddy's," I heard him mumble,
    his voice a choked whisper.
"You'll wear these, Mary," the mother said,
      paying for the sneakers.
  They left, walking out of the store in a cloud
    of resentment and confusion.
I walked down the aisles and I was six again

wanting to wear my father's shoes.
He had a pair of dark brown wingtips...
elegant, strong, smelling of leather
                    and maleness.
I would slip my small feet into them when
                    my mother wasn't looking
                    and just stand, wanting
                    to grow up like him.
I smiled at the memory and saw a pair of wingtips
            on the counter. I carried them over to a bench
            and sat down, ignoring the looks
                    from other customers.
I tried them on and they enveloped my feet
like an old friend's hug.
I paid for them and wore them out, listening
to the steady click of their heels
                    on the floor.

Wondering
Mac McCord

I haven't come this way before, and I stand here,
Half afraid of becoming someone I don't know.
Others have drawn away, even you... or maybe it
Was me who left...
                    Who went looking in the early fog
                        For second stars and chances.
            I'm coming back you know, coming back to you
                        As who I really am... someday.

For Guys Like Me . . .
Rocco Rinaldi Kayiatos

Growing up it's always a struggle
Trying to juggle school
Acting cool
And what I could possibly wear
When I'm in a swimming pool
Don't wanna be the fool when they realize
I got something between my thighs that
They didn't expect
And no one understands or respects people like us
So while I fuss they do the normal
Teenage things
Like plot their future
And I'm never too sure what could happen in
The locker room
But it's safe to assume that there's
Some kind of asshole
And so I'm precocious
Cause they act ferocious
But they're not even scary

Cause I'm a limp wristed/
swift fisted/swishy ass fairy/mary
And they could be the first to suck
My big hairy nuts after the metoidioplasty
I'm gonna blast they asses right out of
The water
You thought I was your daughter
But Mom and Dad
Don't get mad cause now I'm your
Son
And I've only just begun to
Start living without fear.

Growing up in the Bay Area with accepting parents made my coming out as a teenage dyke as natural as it should be for kids everywhere. My family bought me all the gayest books and movies they could get, and were thrilled with my newly proclaimed identity. I reveled in it as well, because it was one more thing that set me apart from the bitches I went to high school with.

I happily labeled myself an "Angry, man-hating, butch dyke!" I would roam the halls, while class was in session, preaching Valerie Solanis's *SCUM Manifesto* until everyone in my town knew me as the angry, man-hating lesbo. And yet I had absolutely no community. No one in my town was gay, at least not outwardly. No one I knew was gay, aside from my Godmother and her dyke lover, but they were much older. It wasn't until I turned nineteen and hit the road with an all-girl traveling poetry show that I even hung out with dykes close to my age. That summer I discovered my community and young queer communities across the US. I finally felt understood, appreciated, desired and connected. I learned that I didn't have to be a misogynist straight boy in a dyke's body to be seen as a boy.

After I returned home, I decided I was surely done hanging around with marginally homophobic straight boys— the traditional company I kept. I wanted my gayness to flourish amongst other fabulous queers. And it has. I feel more queer by the day. I feel as queer as I felt when I was still a little boy. When I used to make everyone call me George and wore my underpants over my clothes. When I would pee standing up with the rest of my male friends. When I would kiss girls and run away, before I understood that I was different. Before puberty hit, and the devastation of breasts and hips, a girl's body, made everything too real. A boy in a girl's body, a girl in a boy's head.

The more trannies I meet, the more I realize a lot of us shared the same childhood. A case of mistaken identity. We always thought that eventually the boy parts would grow in, and we'd just be one of the guys. But they didn't, and we feel challenged by appearances which don't quite fit us. Then it becomes a matter of trying to accept our bodies and own them. Not always an easy task for a 5'3" bio-girl that thinks he's a 6' tall buff Greek male model. But rarely is anyone ever truly satisfied with her or his birth-given bodies.

Now I'm learning to work with what I have (and a low dose of testosterone) to create a body closer to my ideal. The more I come into myself and my body, I begin to realize this vessel is the best gift I could receive. I've been blessed to have my physical form be an educational experience for the rest of the world. It's a truly beautiful existence, riding the line of gender and seeing everything from both a female and male perspective.

I didn't always feel this way. For a good part of my adolescent life all of this was a curse, a cruel joke karma was playing on me. To put me in a body that couldn't even go to a public rest room without incident and explanation. The constant taunting and staring. But I've come to a place where I accept myself and love who I am in the world, this world that is light years away from the consciousness that I inherently possess.

So I understand my struggle and feel gifted that I can encompass both masculinity and femininity and not be defined by my genitalia. One part of me could never be my entire identity. What matters is how I feel and carry myself, who I know I am before I see a mirror. Sometimes I'm shaken out of my reality when a man addresses me as "Baby," or even "Lady," and wonder who they are talking to, or how they could think to call me lady when my hair is a perfectly coifed pompadour and I'm wearing a three-piece suit. I'm no lady, but I'm no man either.

Male To Male
Johnny Giovanni Righini

INSIDE OUT:

As a child, I knew I was different. I was raised in a sheltered environment and told to believe that I was female. This label felt so misrepresenting but at the time I had no idea why. My parents loved to dress me real pretty and sent me to strict religious schools that neglected to teach their students about worldly issues. I never felt like I fit in with any of the other children, which made me constantly feel like an outcast. I felt isolated from them and myself because of my lower genitalia. I use to examine them and wonder why they did not look "right". I paid a lot of attention to this insecurity because I knew something was inaccurate. My genitals were very ambiguous compared to how I was told they should appear. Did I have some kind of birth defect that my parents did not tell me about? The first time I noticed natural lubrication of my genitals I panicked. What was happening to my so-called body and why? My answer to this was a blowdryer jammed up my underwear and crotch, praying that I would not burn myself. I became obsessed with my "drying myself off" ritual every time I got "wet". But that was just the beginning. Sometimes I would sit backwards on the toilet or stand up to urinate because doing this actually made me feel better about my developmental differences. Once in 6th grade my friend and I took ziplock sandwich bags, filled them with water, locked them shut and then placed them into our underwear. Those heavy bags of water created boy bulges inside innocent little girl panties and reassured me of my long lost security. This is the first time I can truly remember feeling power. Something about this power felt so substantially correct.

Reclaiming Myself:

By my late teen years, I began to reclaim this power and myself. I realized the life I had been living was a lie. I was not happy in my own skin and felt there was no point in living. I began to do research on gender identity and found a whole new world in front of me. A world full of possibilities and other people like me; people who were raised as a gender they honestly were not. After intense communication with myself, and endless amounts of soul searching, I started to live full-time as male. What I thought was impossible really wasn't after all; I could fully physically transition to my male body because mentally I had always been there. At 19, I started testosterone hormonal therapy treatment, and by 20 I had my first gender corrective surgery: chest reconstruction.

All this made me feel like I had been reborn. I had never felt so comfortable and liberated. People around me began to acknowledge my new happiness. My mom, whom I've always been close to, noticed it the most. She started to realize that loving me was not about loving the person she wanted me to be, but about loving the person that I am. Her son. Of course, everything was hard for her at first. Transitioning can be very dramatic. My mom and practically the rest of the world assumed I now identified as FTM (female to male) transsexual, but that was a false accusation. First off, I was not going from F to M. Whatever gender my parents chose to raise me was their choice but the gender I truly am is not my choice… It's just who I am, and who I was meant to be. I never felt I was F because I never was, and therefore the FTM identity does me no justice. Recognizing this helped me form my MTM (male to male) identity.

FOREVER FREE:

What is male-to-male? I can only answer this from my personal experience. I believe in making my own definitions and encourage others to do so as well. What MTM means to me does not have to be what MTM means to you. Being male to male has meant evolving into the man that I am. I've done this by breaking society's gender boundaries, boxes, roles, expectations, limits, standards, rules, and stereotypes. I think "birth sex" is pathetic so I've crossed that term out of my daily vocabulary. Sex to me means getting laid!

It's fucked up to even attempt to determine a child's gender at birth. Gender is NOT based on our genitals. We as human beings have the right to claim our own identities, like mine of MTM. It's taken me self-discovery, strength, courage, motivation, faith, and honesty to make it this far. I look at my past life as a performance, a show. I "performed" as the gender I was raised to believe I was, to keep my parents happy. This did not make me happy though. I did it for them back then but NOW is for me. If I had the chance to go back and change my past, I would not. Everything I have gone through has happened for a reason. If things had been different, I would have never got the chance to grow into the man I've become, in the ways that I have. I keep my past life locked away inside a special place in my heart. I have healed and moved on. I am now forever free and able to do my part as a human being on this earth. I believe my main purpose in life is to create change. There are times when I forget how to do this and then I remind myself to just keep doing what I'm doing. That is: being heard, making things happen, stomping on society, promoting social change, learning, teaching, loving, accepting, supporting, staying positive, growing and living in this radical life I call my Revolution.

Father and Son
Mykkah Herner

It's been a long, hard week filled with plenty of trips through the attic (with hundreds of stuffed animals I'd refused to part with over the years), through the church (with piles of clothes for the rummage sale), through memories and former selves. My parents are moving out of the house they've lived in since I was four. At four I was a tomboy – scuffed up knees from climbing trees, holes in all my clothes (especially the dresses Mom made me wear for holidays and church on Sunday), short hair that was just starting to darken from its baby blonde, and a daredevil sentimentality.

At fourteen, I went through my brief girly-girl stage. Well, okay. It lasted four years, five tops. I tried to fit in with all the popular kids, then settled for a clique that was less popular but still very informed by gender roles. My best friend became a guidette – the hair, the nails, the gold jewelry, the mouth – and our boyfriends Pat and Joey were respectively Irish and Italian Catholic. Me? I had long, well-kept hair (except when I was rolling around under neighbors' porches), makeup, and tight-fitting clothes that accentuated my girlish curves (that I didn't really have because I was 120 lbs. and complained a lot about how flat my chest was).

At 24, I was a dyke: vegan, woman-identified, two cats, partner whom I'd moved in with after four months (we were already up to our fourth anniversary!). Very political about gay marriage, animal rights, and the oppression of (gay, white, middle-class, able-bodied) women. Marched in the dyke march, volunteered briefly at the lesbian resource center, was tight with money. I came out to my family – Mom, Dad, sisters, their boyfriends (now husbands), aunts, uncles, cousins – had a commitment ceremony, and demanded respect for my alternative lifestyle. It's a stereotype, but I was the stereotype.

Well, it would seem I've had a busy few years, or maybe that's the nature of going to grad school and learning a lot really fast, being exposed to new information. Four years ago I learned about open relationships and quickly after that s/m and power dynamics.

Three years ago I learned about divorce (shame, humility, failure, and reframing), and gender roles. I TA'ed for a "socialization of gender" class; *Boys Don't Cry* came out. I was given *Mulan* for Xmas. A new class of students joined my program, a few of them bringing an appreciation for queer theory in its attention to gender studies. I started working on my models of non-monogamy (which to me is very different from open relationships). Towards the end of that year I attended my first FTM meeting. It scared the shit out of me; I belonged there in a way. Not entirely, but I had walked in the door!

Two years ago I moved to a more liberal place, concerned that I would shelve any gender questions I had since the only people I knew here were family. I started meeting folks who identified as genderqueer (when forced to identify); folks who were queer in sexuality, and queer in sex and relationships. I learned a lot about other people's models of non-monogamy: how to be a slut and enjoy it; how to share information in a respectful way; the evil J word, jealousy; how to have multiple relationships of various forms in a small community where everyone was or is fucking everyone else. I learned a lot about b/d/s/m: how to play in public; finding and manipulating the power I have as a bottom; playing with multiple people at a time; negotiating, roles. I learned a multiplicity of specific and alternative gender identities: fag, kid, boy, straight teenaged boy.

In the last year I started changing my name to a more masculine, yet still potentially ambiguous, one. I became my Daddy's boy, getting the kid and masculine parts of me validated through validating my Daddy. I quit two jobs that could only see me as a nice butch little lesbian. I started talking with my mom a bit about gender. We talk on intellectual rather than personal levels, but I suspect that she gets me. My 2-year-old nephew has taken to calling me 'Uncle' and generally I've been just moving around the world as a non-girl.

I am very aware and conscious of what it can mean for those who identify as "girl" to hear me saying I'm not it – and it's important enough to me to make it part of my body text, not a footnote. I had a great conversation with a femme friend who felt hurt. I explained that I loved the way femininity worked for her – she did it well. On me? Well, it was like those dresses my mom made me wear – I just kept poking holes in them, trying to make them more comfortable, but ultimately they just didn't fit right.

So today marks the last day of an exhausting week of hiding a self, one that feels right, from my family. There's just one more thing to clean out: my dad's closet. He's using me as an excuse to get things organized for the move. He's used to me stealing his button-down shirts. The 14 to 19-year-old took them as a thin girl looking sexy in men's clothes. The 20 to 25-year-old did it as a dyke wearing intentionally more ambiguous clothing styles, saving money and finding clothes that hid a growing body. The 28-year-old is hoping to find some nice dress shirts and casual shirts that my dad has recently outgrown with his beer belly and lack of neck, but should fit me well. He starts very tentatively, pulling out a shirt or two from three or four sizes ago. I am wearing my tightest binder (but it's not nearly as flattening as I want it to be) and a T-shirt over which I will try his old button-down shirts. These shirts are a bit tight across my chest and I make a funny face. We put them in the "for the church" pile.

He moves to the two or three sizes ago set and they start fitting. He pulls out a casual wool overshirt   off white with thick red and yellow horizontal stripes – and smiles sweetly at the shirt. "I used to love this shirt…" He frowns, holding the hangered shirt in his hands. He looks at me and his eyes show a glimmer of hope for a minute; then he holds it out to me. Knowing it won't fit exactly like I'll want it to, I slip it off the hanger and onto my shoulders. A little tight around the chest, a little itchy, but I look just like my dad. I put it in the "mine" pile and we smile. He starts pulling the shirts out quicker and quicker. We're both breaking a sweat. The "mine" pile is getting larger than the "for the church" pile. I'm excited just to have new clothes. Well, not JUST that.

My dad looks at me for a minute, I'm trading one shirt for the next – smiling at his likeness in the mirror. He reaches deep into his closet and pulls out a suit. One of the older ones – and one of his favorites. He looks confused for a minute, then plops it on the bed between the "for the church" and "mine" piles. He shrugs and says, "Wanna try any suits?" I jump and flip inside. Free suits? From my dad? That might actually fit? Last time I tried on suits it was with two queer boys I was fucking/dating/friends with and together they only outweighed me by a little. I cried then, but now I'm giddy and my dad can see it.

The first one doesn't fit, but there are plenty more. Some come with little stories. Some still have his suspenders attached. Some are clearly sentimental favorites. "Hey, do you want tails?" he asks excitedly at one point. Sadly, the tails don't fit. He tries on the pants of most of the suits, to make sure they don't possibly, just maybe fit, just this once still, but then hands them over with what I sense to be relief in his eyes. For the first time in his life he is willingly and intentionally passing down his clothes to someone, to his child, to me. And then it hits me – we're having our first father-son bonding moment, only he doesn't know it.

I mean, sure, we went to baseball games when I was little, but that was different – he could justify that by saying, "kids like games," "kids like sports," or the feminist twist from my mom "girls like sports, too." But this has no other explanation. He is handing down his suits to me and I am excitedly accepting, appreciating, and celebrating them.

Then he does something new. He opens up his dresser drawers and tries on some casual clothes that he wears around the house. Some of them fit him – when he sucks it in. But he has me try them on anyway, saying, "They'll be more comfortable on you." They are.

By the time I get on the airplane I have an extra borrowed suitcase full of my dad's hand-me-downs and he can tell just by remembering how long ago he was able to wear something whether or not it will fit me. I've said goodbye to a lot of the younger selves I had visited during the week. I haven't talked to my family about gender roles (the only unchecked box on my to-do list), but I've learned a lot about how to be a son.

Learning To Be Gay
Matthew Kalley

Having spent over four decades of my life as a heterosexual female, I was, at age forty-two, about as prepared to enter the gay community as a Hollywood actor is to be president of the United States. But, having witnessed the latter, I was fairly certain I could take on the challenge—if I could only get past the question that seemed to be popping up again and again from well-meaning but curious friends: "Why would you transition to become a gay man?"

It was never my intention to "become a gay man." It happened that way because male hormones morphed my body faster than the full moon transformed Lon Chaney. Almost overnight, I became the poster boy for the "Gay is Not a Choice" campaign when my appearance changed but my attractions did not. Although I was lacking the equipment necessary to become a fully functioning gay man (at least one who goes to bathhouses), I knew that I would have to become culturally competent if I was to function (translation: get laid) at all. Fortunately, I had a variety of gay male friends who were concerned about my future sex life—not concerned enough to offer themselves up for the cause, but more than willing to give me a few pointers along the way.

It started with wardrobe. If my friends were to be believed, clothes not only make the gay man, they get him made as well. I didn't know where to begin, but I soon learned what not to do with the help of my buddy, Eric.

"That guy's not gay," Eric pointed out as we watched an attractive man walk by. "He's not coordinated. Gay men are very big on matching." Whew. I was glad I learned that one early on. As a female, I thought that any colors went together as long as the fashion magazines said they did. I spent a painful adolescence in "mustard" and "eggplant" and lived through the disco era in neon green and screaming purple. Now I had to match and the pressure was on. After several daunting trips to the men's department and a few too-close-for-comfort encounters in the dressing room, I finally settled on what is now my current wardrobe—blue jeans and black T-shirts. They make several statements, including "Hey, I don't have breasts" and "I don't know what the hell to wear." Not especially profound but as long as they're yelling the first one and whispering the second, I really don't care what they say.

Even though I've found my look, I sometimes continue in my frustrating quest for gay style, staring in the mirror with disgust and asking myself these questions:

"Why don't I look good in a baseball cap?"

"Why can't I afford a T-shirt with the designer's name printed on the front?"

"Does this sweater make me look fat?"

"Do these blacks go together?"

Of course, these are the same questions I asked myself as a female (with the exception of the one about the baseball cap). Remembering the straight men I used to date is of little help. They didn't pay much attention to what they wore. They didn't even try on clothes at the store. They'd just grab a pair of 32-34s or whatever waist size they had eaten themselves into, and whip out the credit card. Then they'd go home, throw the pants in the washer and dryer, take them out wrinkled and pull them on with a T-shirt that said, "Women love me, fish fear me." After this, they were ready to go anywhere. It was embarrassing to be walking next to them, but I could take consolation in the fact that, no matter what I wore, I looked good in comparison.

In my jeans and T-shirts I sometimes feel like a fashion disaster next to my gay male friends, who seem to know exactly what the next trend will be and some secret place to purchase it. They also never iron things. It makes me wonder if there's some permanent press gene I don't know about   one that makes guys lust for other guys while maintaining a sharp, even crease in their khakis. I can iron for hours only to achieve the semi-rumpled, slept-in look which I then pretend is sexy—I look like I just got out of bed. Unfortunately, no one ever asks if I'd like to get back in. This does, however, keep me from worrying about whether or not my underwear is erotic enough. I don't think it is. It's white. But it goes with everything.

Clothing turned out to be only one part of the equation and, apparently, the least important. Jeans and a T-shirt don't look any worse than a Prada suit when they're in a heap on the bedroom floor. As I continued to mainline testosterone, I had more and more desire to see that Prada suit, or any other male window dressing, on the floor rather than on the man. I soon discovered that, in the absence of the real thing, porn was the way to go. I'd seen enough straight porn to know that doughy, balding men and drop-dead gorgeous women were not going to do it for me, but I figured gay porn had to be different. I eventually broached the subject with my friends, Jeff and Aaron, who were more than willing to let me sample their collection.

They decided to surprise me while I was sitting on their bed flipping through the gay equivalent of *Playboy*, which featured men not found anywhere in nature. Jeff casually put a tape into the VCR and hit play. When I began watching, they both left the room, evidently to give me some privacy to do what I would never do in a friend's bedroom at four in the afternoon. It was possible that they mistook my fascination with the "plot" for lust. My interest soon turned to amusement as I watched a copulating couple turn into a many-car steam locomotive as, one by one, other men happened upon this act and wordlessly joined in. I found it curious because if I were to enter a bedroom where two of my friends were having sex, I don't think I would simply walk up and insert my Tab A into the first available Slot B. Instead, I would quietly excuse myself, close the door, then scramble into the next room where I could listen through the wall.

I later found other pornography that I appreciated more than the mechanical inner workings of an X-rated Swiss clock. Perhaps it's my straight upbringing, but I am much fonder of one-on-one, where sexy, muscled men actually kiss, fondle and caress each other in a prelude to the really nasty stuff. All in all, even given my selective aesthete, gay porn eventually proved to be a complete turn-on and a definite feast for the eye. Getting it, however, was another matter.

While I was still in the adolescent stage of porn procurement, my friends helpfully took me to a gay video store and introduced me to the owner in hopes that I would start checking out my own movies and quit borrowing theirs. I was horrified that the clerk would know what I was going to do with those videos behind closed doors.

"Aren't you embarrassed that he knows you're going home to jerk off to these?" I asked Aaron. He looked at me as if I'd only been a guy for a very short time.

"No," he said. "The clerk does it, too. Everybody does it."

Everybody may do it, but in the straight world, nobody talks about it and Pee Wee Herman got arrested for it. That kind of socialization makes it tough to suddenly switch gears and do it in your friends' bedroom at four in the afternoon when you can hear them in the living room discussing which wine to open for dinner. Although I was eventually able to admit to what I did when I watched porn, I was still thirsting for reality.

The problem with getting exactly what I wanted, though, was that other guys tended to want the same thing. They had it. I didn't. My friend Paul, who took me on a tour of the gay bar scene, insisted that I was lucky. I was skeptical, but he explained that my small earlobes, thumbs and nose could work in my favor. According to Paul, these are the markers that men look for when determining the possible size of other, less visible, appendages. If a man happened to be interested in me after a wily examination of my ears, face and hands, then he probably wasn't a size queen. A size queen? I was hoping for a microbiologist—or at least someone who collected miniatures. As I moved from mainstream to manhood, I became increasingly aware of the importance of size in gay male courtship rituals, i.e., personal ads. After weeks of study, I finally realized that 8-1/2 inches had nothing to do with new snow on the ski slopes. I decided it was a gay thing. I had seen my share of male organs in my lifetime and I knew that 8-1/2 inches didn't exist in the straight world, as much as my ex-boyfriends would want me to insist that I had personally experienced it.

The problem with this size obsession is that, unlike breast implants (the female heterosexual remedy for the size-impaired), there is no truly viable method available to men to help them "measure up" to the demands of the personals. I can't let that bother me or I'd be in a permanent state of depression, but it must be difficult for some factory-equipped guys. I think Paul wanted my sympathy when he relayed a sob story about being in a hot tub with a gorgeous man who got "shortchanged" by nature. While he lamented over his disappointment, I marveled over the incredible luck of being naked with a heart-stopping hunk. What could he possibly have to complain about? Now I like penises as much as the next guy, but what I like even more are the men who are attached to them, who also come in different sizes. Along with the infinite variety available, I wouldn't rule anyone out based on the calculations of a tape measure—although I'm still waiting for "Mr. 8-1/2 Inches" to wedge himself into my, um, heart.

While I enjoyed my Gay 101 classes, I still don't have my Ph.D. and probably never will. After several years of being male, I've given up on the idea of fitting into any particular mold in any particular community. Now, if I walk down the street holding hands with a man, the world believes I'm gay. Several years ago, the same world saw me as straight. So what I really learned while learning to be gay is that if a person is sexually oriented to men, that person isn't gay unless he himself is a man. Straight, gay—they're just labels, based not on the gender a person is attracted to but on the gender that person is. I didn't change my sexual orientation, I only changed my label. That hasn't been a problem for me. My only complaint is that none of my labels say Prada.

Transitioning
or
What's a Nice Dyke Like Me Doing Becoming a Gay Guy?
Gavriel Alejandro Levi Ansara

If stereotypical Western Anglo (which isn't my culture anyway) masculinity was a requirement of belonging to the man club, my Dad and all of my male relatives would be kicked out. I don't see "being a man" as anything related to being masculine or feminine, any more than I see "being a woman" as being feminine or masculine. There are many butch women, femme men, women who fix cars, men who like to sew, etc. I don't equate femininity with femaleness, or the desire to be a woman.

One of the reasons it took me years to finally come out to myself as FTM is that I was convinced that I was just a different kind of woman. Yeah, women can be butch, femme, masculine, feminine, fix cars, wear men's clothes, etc. But I'm not one, and I never have been. Only now that I'm recognizing my identity do I feel comfortable with my own femininity, which is closer to flaming queen... I have always hated femininity because it made people force me into the female category, which didn't fit. As a man, I can embrace both femininity and masculinity in myself, without feeling that I'm being forced into some box that isn't me.

I tried to be happy as a butch woman, but the woman part simply wasn't me. I think it is sad that even the most enlightened people seem to think that gender stereotypes are what makes people want to transition. I used to be guilty of that myself, when hearing about the decisions of my trans friends. In fact, my belief that only sexists would want to transition was the main reason why I fought so hard against coming out to myself and anyone else. In fact, it's the notion that anyone who transitions is antifeminist and patriarchal which kept me from dealing with this for so many years. I have never wanted breasts. I've always secretly felt most comfortable picturing my anatomy as male. It's that simple. I have never related to women's issues about their bodies, and I have always related to men's.

For sure, there are many other ways to be than the binary genders. And there are people who really don't fit any gender paradigm. A startling majority of my previous female partners are now transitioning or identify as FTM. I was a butch who was attracted to other butches, but there was always something clandestine lurking beneath the surface. My lovers and I always called each other male terms in bed, never questioning the fact that we referred to each other's female genitalia as "cocks." Our secrets were a guilty pleasure for which we castigated ourselves by attending numerous lesbian rallies. Our other lesbian friends did not share our secret, because they were truly satisfied as women. It took most of us years to figure out that we weren't butch dykes, as we had originally thought, but something else entirely. I forced myself for years to jack off thinking of my body as female, but before I came, I would always switch back to my body as male. It was a private sin, something which I tried to beat out of myself at great personal cost because I believed it was not feminist not to love my body as it was. Now I see that the only truly antifeminist thing is not letting people be whomever they are inside.

Acceptance begins with the self before it can extend to others. I am a strong feminist and I will always be one. I am transitioning not because I hate women, but because I love myself. I am transitioning not because I think men and women have different characteristics, because I am emphatically NOT a gender essentialist. I am transitioning because I feel most comfortable when people refer to me in male terms and because I feel most comfortable and liberated in my body as a man. Being a woman is beautiful, and some people born male want more than anything to live as one. I just don't. I shudder to think of friends and acquaintances that see me as someone who has stereotypical ideas about gender, when that's the opposite of everything for which I stand. Many of my friends have asked me with tense awe if I am going to have "the operation." The only operation required for this journey is one described so eloquently by Bob Marley, that of "emancipating yourself from mental slavery." I emancipate myself not only from the mental slavery of finite destinations but from the notion that there is a single path to happiness. I'll make my journey with the rational, methodical, and intensive thought which characterizes responsible life decisions. There could be many reasons to remain closeted or to continue to evade attempts at personal discovery. But there are even more reasons to transition.

My desire for happiness and peace of mind is mine.

Once More... With Feeling
Dean Spade

Lately my life is about pronoun enforcement. It's one of my primary social occupations. How did things end up this way? How paradoxical: my trans project is about destroying rigid gender classifications and occupying multiple, contradictory subject positions and non-cohesive gender characteristics but I spend enormous amounts of time enforcing 'he'. Have I turned into a dreaded gender defender? No, but everyday I'm forced to confront the fact that most people—even people I expect to demonstrate thrilled excitement about the work I'm doing with my own body and mind and the minds of others to destabilize gender—can't handle calling someone 'he' whom they used to call 'she', or who doesn't look like a boy to them. Of course, if you're with me, you start noticing that no one and everyone looks like a boy. So when I ask to be called 'he,' these are the things I get back, all from people I truly believe have good intentions and would say they support me and trans people generally.

Category 1: burden shifting. Two versions exist. The first occurs when I meet someone and inform them that I prefer the pronouns 'he', 'him', and 'his'. They say something like, 'That's hard,' or 'You'll have to be patient with me,' or 'Correct me when I mess up.' The second version is the person who has known me for a while and knows I go by 'he' but continually uses 'she' when referring to me. When reminded, they say 'C'mon, I'm trying' or 'C'mon, I get it right most of the time.'

These people are telling the truth. It is very hard to transform pronouns into a conscious process instead of an assumption based on social signals that have been instilled since birth. However, their willingness to fail at the difficult task of active thinking where non-thinking has existed is not okay. It is inexcusably shortsighted to look at this lack of consciousness only from an individualized perspective of arduousness, rather than recognizing it as a socio-political condition imposed upon everyone. It's understandable to feel daunted when coming up against a new and challenging concept and use of language, but it's not okay to refuse critical engagement and expect those whose identity positions you foreclose to be infinitely patient.

There is neither innocence nor insignificance to the mistake of 'she' for 'he' when referring to a person who has chosen to take on a 'wrong' pronoun. Even if it is done thoughtlessly, that thoughtlessness comes from and supports the two cardinal rules of gender: that all people must look like the specific gender (male or female) they are called by, and that gender is fixed and cannot be changed. Each time this burden shifting occurs, the non-trans person affirms these gender rules, informing me that they will not do the work to see the world outside of these rules.

In addition—and this is where the burden shifting becomes apparent—by expecting that they will always be corrected when they err, and that I should only reasonably anticipate part-time compliance with my preferred pronoun, it is ensured that the burden of breaking the rules remains with me. In reality, by implementing the rules which instruct them to call people who look like a girl, 'she', they burden me with the rules of gender fixation. This effectively makes the problems arising from others' confusion about perceived gender the isolated responsibility of the confusing person—the trans person—rather than a result of a diabolically rigid gender system that screws over everyone's ability to fully inhabit their lives.

Often the people who offer burden-shifting responses identify with feminist politics, and would agree in principle that gender rigidity and hierarchy is terrible and that people should be able to change their individual gender positions, identification, and redefine the meaning of traditional gender identifications. However, they still let me know, when they pass the burden of how hard it is for them to remember or how they get it right most of the time, that what I'm asking them to do and rethink may be too much to expect. It isn't. It is possible to change how you think about pronouns. It's confusing and wonderful and totally fucks up your ability to navigate dichotomous gender easily. That is the point. If you aren't confused and frustrated by using words like 'he' and 'she' to label everyone in the world, then you should be working harder.

Category two: to be a trans victim. A popular response to complaints about pronoun enforcement is a sympathetic discourse about respect. I got this from quite a few people after the Gay Shame fiasco where I was introduced on stage as 'she' before I spoke. Many of the wonderful people who were also outraged by this described it as an issue of respect and of not making a trans safe space at Gay Shame (an activist event held in opposition to Gay Pride's commercialism). Though there is a respect problem and it does in fact make the space unsafe for trans people, this approach individualizes the problem to trans people. When I hear non-trans people say that I should be called by the pronoun I choose as a matter of respecting my choice, it borders on a tolerance argument. As if trans people are somehow different people, and when they come around you should respect their difference, but do no more. This lines up with a view that all 'different' people, whether disabled, old, immigrant, of color, trans, gay, etc., should be 'respected' by calling them what they want, but that the fundamental fact of their difference and of the existence of a norm should not be analyzed.

Often this view accompanies a perspective of these different people as victims, pathetic outsiders who others should smile at and might be honored with a special day at work or school when we all discuss how difference is good.

I'm not looking for people to mindlessly force themselves to call me 'he' in order to avoid making me uncomfortable. If comfort was my goal, I could probably have found a smoother path than the one I'm on, right? The word 'he' wasn't chosen because it means something true to me, or feels all homey and delicious. No pronoun feels personal. I've chosen it because the act of saying 'he', of looking at the body I'm in and the way that my gender has been identified since birth, disrupts oppressive processes that fix gender as real, immutable, and determinative of one's station in life. I'm not hoping that people will see that I'm different, paste a fake smile on their faces and force themselves to say some word without thought. I'm hoping that they will feel implicated, that it will make them think about the realness of everyone's gender, that it will make them feel more like they can do whatever they want with their gender, or at least cause a pause where one normally would not exist. Quite likely, this will be uncomfortable for all of us, but I believe that becoming uncomfortable with the oppressive system of rigid gender assignment is a great step toward undoing it.

So, go ahead; try thinking outside the confines of 'tolerance' taught by the diversity training you were given at college or work or on TV. Challenge yourself to do more than mimic respectful behavior that will make 'different people' feel at home. Instead, take a look at what those differences mean, how they got invented, what they are based on, and how they determine behavior, power, access, and language. Respect and safe space are a good start and a hard-fought accomplishment, but I certainly fantasize about a more engaged approach to difference.

My Life as a Boy: The Early Years
Eli Wadley

I started off my life as a boy at a slight disadvantage, nothing so big that it could not be overcome with a little ingenuity and spunk, but a setback, nonetheless. You see, despite being a little boy from the very start destined to become the handsome and talented man I am today, I happened to have had the unexpected surprise of being born a girl. I've yet to come across a reasonable explanation for this mix-up, but there's no sense crying over spilt milk.

My inner boy showed up early on, when I clobbered the little neighbor boy with my Raggedy Ann doll to get at his Tonka dump truck. I sealed the deal when I gave myself (and all the dolls in my bedroom) matching crewcuts. From that point on there was no turning back. My personal preferences did not necessarily match up with what my parents expected from their precious little princess: long braids, pigtails, flowing locks? No. Bikini halter tops, rainbow terrycloth tube tops? No. Hot pink sweatshirt with sparkly kitty applique? NO. Cut-off shorts and no shirt? Yes. Tree climbing, basketball, ice hockey? Of course. Playing tea party and house? No, no, no. Cowboys and gladiators at Halloween? Yes. Fairy princess with tiara and glittering wand? Absolutely not. Handbags, make-up kits, and nail polish? Not really. Backpacks, toolkits, and fake scar and bruise sets? That's more like it!

My dad indulges me, teaches me how to use the tools in his woodshop, takes me fishing, and allows me to buy a pocketknife with a molded plastic fake wood handle with my allowance from my favorite hangout... the hardware store. My mom, operating on the assumption that she has a daughter and not a son, buys me opal clip-on earrings for my birthday even though I asked for a chemistry set. Mom buys clothes and leaves them on my bed for me to find after school. Piles of stiff scratchy lacy white shirts with scalloped collars, soft pastel sweaters with tiny ribbons tied in bows on the neck, houndstooth scooter skirts, wooden clogs and rainbow legwarmers, a pink satin rollerskating jacket (think fourth grade version of Olivia Newton John in *Xanadu*). It's not much to work with, but I do what I can to adapt this pink and fluffy wardrobe to my boyhood needs. A big black belt here, a pair of ratty sneakers there. Cutting off sleeves to make sweater vests and tucking frilly skirts into the Sears Toughskins I wear underneath can go a long way towards achieving that boyish look. I also find it useful to carefully cut each of my dresses and skirts into four separate pieces.

Hair is always an issue. I personally preferred to sport the style John Denver was wearing during his golden years. But my mother, unfortunately, was more inspired by the hairstyles of America's sweethearts... Dorothy Hamill and Shirley Temple. I like to think all the failed home permanents my mother tried to give me were due to my hair's unflinching loyalty. My hair knew I was no Shirley Temple and it was not going to just lie there and let her send a little boy out into the world in sausage curls and ringlets. One year my mother actually asks the hairdresser to give me a Farrah Fawcett-style hairdo a la *Charlie's Angels*. The old battle axe hairdresser puffs out her cigarette smoke at my mother and barks, "That ain't no hairstyle suited for a little boy." I cross my arms and give my mother a smug self-satisfied look.

Colors were also a challenge. Why something as simple as a blue ski cap could send my mother into apoplectic fits has always been beyond me, but apparently other mothers had similar triggers. My best friend, Hap, has a red denim jacket that matches his red denim jeans so I get Mom to buy me a white set just like his. We wear our suits all summer long and like cool dudes we take off our t-shirts and wear the jackets over smooth naked boy chests as we light fires in the field behind my house. The invitation to his birthday party comes in the mail and it is pink, the ink letters of my name smeared and water-stained. Mom tells me this story she thinks is so funny as we open the invitation together. Hap wanted to give me a blue invitation but his mom won't let him since, after all, I was a girl. They argued, voices raised, and he just refused to believe her. He cried and cried as his mom made him write his best buddy's name on a pink envelope. Mom snorts as she laughs, saying, "Whoever heard of a boy named Elise?!" She laughs till she cries.

I have an unbounded enthusiasm for running and jumping and playing hard that mysteriously vanishes into thin air as soon as I enter the girls' gym. I'm fast and coordinated and competitive but I can't seem to pull off the girl jock thing. They are majestic foxy girl athletes: long limbs, smooth rosy skin, clean sweet-smelling ponytails, strong, graceful and somehow able to look proportionate in the goofy gym uniforms we are forced to wear. I, on the other hand, look like a stringy spaz with scabs on my knees and dirt smudges on my face. I seem to be mostly legs and elbows and giant eyeglasses. I do not look quite right in the short blue polyester gym shorts and yellow T-shirt with a sticky blue image of our school mascot, a snarling cougar, pressed on the front. It does not help that I find them excruciatingly attractive and unattainable. This makes me self-conscious and clumsy. They are gazelles and I am a weird hybrid of chimpanzee and puppy.

I tend to get a lot of crap I prefer to avoid. You know the drill, the very loud public discussion amongst my peers, teachers, and parents: Are you a boy or a girl? You wanna be a boy or what? You need to act like a young lady, young lady. Girls don't act like that. Sit like a lady, please. Put your legs together and sit up straight. Hey, stay out of the boys' clothes section, we're not shopping for your brother today. You can have the pink bike, but not the blue one. Blue is for boys. You run fast for a girl. If you are a girl, why do you look like a boy? You look so much better in pastels, honey. Dark colors are for boys. Oh, honey, you could be so pretty, why do you have to try so hard to look unattractive? No one is going to want to marry you when you grow up if you don't try to be pretty.

Photos of me... a boy in a dress, stiff, embarrassed, humiliated. Early drag but without the sequins, feather boas, and definitely without the glamour. I would not relive those years even if you paid me one million dollars. Well, except for this one: third grade lunchroom. The girl across the table is looking over her chocolate milk carton at me while she drinks. Every time I look at her she giggles and looks away. I'm feeling a flush of embarrassment creep up my face. She leans over and whispers to her friend and they both laugh and look over at me again. I am used to being the dork so I know it is something about my clothes or hairdo, or maybe I have food in my teeth, but I still can't get used to kids laughing at me. I'm shifting around in my seat, trying to find a place to rest my eyes, trying to hold down the blush with sheer willpower and not succeeding. I prepare myself for the worst case scenario when I realize her friend is about to say something to me. She leans across the table and says, "My friend thinks you're cute. That you'd be cute if you were a boy." Milk carton girl elbows her friend's ribs and they both start to giggle uncontrollably. I feel strangely happy and smile a big goofy smile at my admirers. Then we go back to eating lunch. My moment to bask in the sun of crushed-out girls has come and gone for the moment. But I'll remember it forever. Like every other boy's first brush with romance.

Living La Vida Medea
Reid Vanderburgh

I was 39 years old, living as a lesbian, when I first realized I'd probably be happier living as a guy. I did not take kindly to this realization, for several reasons. First, I had quite a life built up in the Portland, Oregon lesbian community. I was a founding member of nine years' standing of the Portland Lesbian Choir, and leaving that group was not on my horizon.

Second, I had a family of choice with whom my bonds were stronger than those with my biological family. All were lesbians. All were fellow Choir members, or members of my mixed chorus, Bridges Vocal Ensemble, or members of both. Queer folks find family as we are able, and often the bonds forged through living in a hostile society are stronger than the bonds of blood connection. I was scared of my realization – if I became a man, would I lose my family of choice?

Finally, I had a negative reaction to the idea of being trans because I had absorbed a mainstream belief that being trans was weird, sick, and perverted. Whenever I did see someone obviously trans, I felt uneasy and off-balance, as if I was in the presence of someone who was psychotic or not fully human. I had some vague notion of "transsexual" and "drag queen" as synonymous terms, which of course had made it impossible for me to recognize myself as a transsexual earlier in my life. I've loathed feminine clothing for as long as I can remember, which is hardly the attitude of a drag queen!

I'd never had conscious fantasies about being male. I had just never felt completely at home in my skin as a female, which caused a low-grade anxiety and depression that was growing steadily as I aged. I hated women's bathrooms. I did not like introducing myself to others, as my former name was highly feminine. I avoided describing myself as a lesbian, and felt vaguely uncomfortable referring to myself as a woman. I had never visited an ob/gyn in my life. I was full of contradictions and felt an enigma to myself – not an easy life for a Virgo.

I would probably still be living in denial had my then-partner not come out to me in the spring of 1995, telling me one night, "I've always felt like a man inside." This effectively held a mirror to my soul. I could no longer ignore what I saw there, but was not prepared to face it. The effect was rather like a badly done substance abuse intervention. Because of the negative attitudes I'd internalized about what it meant to be trans, I had a difficult time feeling okay about the concept of going through female-to-male transition.

Then one day a bisexual friend said to me, with some envy in her voice, "What a gift, to be able to live as both sexes in one lifetime." This one phrase reframed the experience for me, for the first time putting a positive spin on the concept of being trans. Nowhere else had I encountered a positive interpretation of what it might mean to be trans. I moved forward with a great deal more confidence and excitement at the possibilities inherent in the unexpected opportunity life had presented me.

I postponed my physical transition for nearly two years, waiting for the Portland Lesbian Choir to record its first CD. I spent those two years in gender limbo-land, being seen primarily as male in my undergrad classes at Portland State University (unless I opened my mouth to speak), being seen as in transition at work, and being seen as a lesbian during Choir rehearsals. I felt the split keenly, never being able to quite integrate these various aspects of my life into one cohesive whole, despite the fact that I came out to everyone who was important to me. Transition cannot be done in the closet.

Once I began hormones and had top surgery, life became much simpler, as my former lesbian life faded away gradually. However, what I found is that I did not become more male in my outlook on life. I became fully male in appearance, while retaining many of the values I'd learned in the lesbian community. I did not feel much more comfortable calling myself a man than I had calling myself a woman, or a lesbian, though I felt fine calling myself a guy and definitely felt more comfortable in my own skin. I did not lose my lesbian family of choice, and found those friendships have retained their original intimacy. If anything, they are deeper than ever, as I am more centered and thus more capable of truly intimate relationships.

I gradually came to realize that I had not transitioned from female to male. I had transitioned from female to not female. In the ensuing years, I have come to agree with Kate Bornstein, a transwoman writer and performer, who stated in her book, *Gender Outlaw,* "I know I'm not a man – about that much I'm very clear, and I've come to the conclusion that I'm probably not a woman, either."

I wasn't raised to be a man. I did not absorb male socialization. I did not have testosterone dominant in my body, with the resulting imperious sex drive, until I was 41 years old. I have never thought of women as other than my equal, and don't believe I can. I don't have any of the traditional attitudes considered male in this society. While I am *capable* of having a monotone discussion about sports, I'd *rather* have a passionate conversation about life.

I've become increasingly convinced, both through personal experience and through conversations with other trans people, that it's not really possible to transition fully from one sex to another. Bio men (men who were born male) see me as a man, though they quickly come to realize there's something not quite man-like about me. Many assume this must mean I'm gay (I don't identify as such), as the thought never enters their minds that perhaps I wasn't always male. Those bio-men who know I'm trans sometimes utilize me as a resource for understanding women's ways of seeing the world, though I have always been treated respectfully by these men.

Bio women see me as a man, though they quickly come to realize there's something not quite man-like about me. Women, however, tend to feel completely comfortable with me in a way many bio-men do not – they subconsciously recognize me as one of them, though not in a way that makes me feel uncomfortable. It does not feel as if they are seeing me as a woman. Rather, they seem to recognize me as a safety zone, a refuge from other men of whom they feel they must be wary. I've had a number of bio-women comment with surprise on how comfortable they feel with me. Many of them, unaware that I'm trans, assume this must mean I'm gay. Because the mainstream view still equates "drag queen" with "transsexual", I've never met a bio-man or bio-woman yet who has figured out on their own that I was born female.

Now I feel I'm neither man nor woman, though the limitations of English force me to choose sides, if only so I may have terminology with which to describe myself. So, I'm a guy, much more comfortable with male pronouns than female, but not really feeling like a man. I'm living *la vida medea* – life in the middle. I have not crossed the bridge from "female" on one side, over an immeasurable chasm, to become "male" on the other side. Rather, I have *become* the bridge.

Moving Into Body
Captain Snowdon

When they finally let me move back into my body
the place was a disaster
holes punched in the walls
burn marks in the carpet
what gives them the right to thrash it so
who needs to know that they handed it back to me
at 4:59 on a friday of a long weekend
Firecracker thank yous
and goodbyes
exile
look you are dying right now
as I return again to my body
shocked at the condition of the wreckage
15.00 will get you through the next 6 hours
after 27 hours in jail sweating, puking
believe in the beginning of the end of all belief
make the hot hot promise of the long sleep
seem better than the finest heroin.

Then I won't have to be your hell
and my own entertainment
yes always open the flood gates to more yes's
no I can't watch you die along with the rest of us
sleep now the time is coming to ache
the weight of chromosomes
bleed
a revolution of manipulation sighs and begins

If Nancy Were A Boy
Captain Snowdon

If Nancy were a boy
he would arrive at my door
Unannounced at 3 a.m.
with a cock in his coat pocket
and a bulge in his jeans
If Nancy were a boy
he would rub his hand
on his crotch
and tell me he could not sleep
"Could he please come in?"
If Nancy were a boy
I would lick his scars
touch his new boy places
with my new boy hands
brandish all my weapons
If Nancy were a boy
I would meet him at the bathhouse
& invite him to my high school reunion
where we would grind slowly to Soft Cell
and drink only champagne

Dear Breasts
Storm Florez

Dear Breasts,

If I had you surgically removed, would you: a) feel abandoned, b) haunt me, c) notice? There's not much of you there, but I'm sure I'd miss you. I might miss you when my lover forgets and grabs for you to find nothing but her own disappointment. I might miss you when I have a baby and there's nothing on me for hir to feed on. The thing is, I feel very confused about you. People look at my face, then for you, to see what I am. They look to see if you're there, right as they're saying Sir to me. Yet they're still not sure what I am.

"Sir, you're in the wrong line." The only time they think they're sure is when my shirt is off and they make me cover you. "Ma'am, I'm going to have to ask you to put your shirt back on." I don't know which way to go. I don't really want to bind you down. I won't wear a bra. I just want to wear a t-shirt all by itself. I want to stop confusing people because confusing people feels dangerous. I think I'd rather them assume that you're not there and that you never were.

Does this make you sad? It makes me sad. Does it make

sense to keep you if I try to hide you? I can love you. Can I set you free? Would you understand? Would I? Would I feel more comfortable in the world? Would I ever be asked to cover you again? Would I still be in danger? Would I be in more danger? Would I be more dangerous? Would my mother notice? You're so small. I wonder who would miss you. Would you haunt me in my dreams, in my waking, in my sex? Would you appear in visions trying to find your way back to me from the pile of fatty tissue in the biohazard bin? I could keep you in a jar of formaldehyde on my altar, or in my freezer. I could take you out of my freezer and introduce you to new lovers so they don't miss out on you entirely.

I could have a fundraiser. I could film the surgery for an art project. I could project the surgery onto the wall while reading *Our Bodies, Ourselves* to an audience. We could be famous! My dear breasts, I could continue to bind you and itch and slouch. I could just be happy with the body that god gave me. I could change the world instead of myself. But as they say, Think Globally, Act Locally. When I think or speak of this, I think I might be hurting you, but you love torture. Or is it me who loves to have you tortured? For all I know, you hate to be clamped and bruised. For all I know this letter could be an answer to your deepest prayers. This is not a goodbye letter. I'm just trying to understand you and me, and why we're here together in this lifetime. Maybe in a past life, I was your hands and you were my one true love. This is a love letter. Talk to me.

GenderFusion
Juan-Alejandro Lamas

GenderFusion: The (he)art of physically, mentally and spiritually fusing one's gender with education, self-knowledge, and passion. The state of fusing oneself into a singular physical body. An occurrence that involves the production of a union of the self.

I coined the term "Genderfusion" to describe my past, present and seemingly permanent condition. Genderfusion is the polar opposite of the supposed GenderCONfusion the medical establishment, gender theorists and binary-focused people think I am suffering from.

I've not been one for theories and, until recently, not one for much of anything I couldn't see or apply physically. Coming from a working class, non-English-speaking, first-generation-attending-school type family, I've been one for action, self-sufficiency, survival, passion, and the ability to be open-minded. Ability is the key word here, meaning I have not always been open-minded nor am I always so, but I do—now more than ever—work on it, harder than ever. I have to. It's the nature of what I am and how I have evolved. Being me leaves not much room for intolerance or judgment of others, for my very existence in humanity, sexuality, gender, religion, law abiding-ness, and daily survival makes me one of the first to go should any intolerance occur. A freak, an abnormal, a deviant, sick: a queer in the truest sense of the word. I never set out to be these things, am I these things? Does calling me those things make it so?

Hence Genderfusion! I grew up in a strict, Spanish-speaking, Catholic home. In the beginning all I knew was the hard work of my parents, their toughness, their struggles, their love, their fights. There were 13 of us living in a three-bedroom home. Parents in one bedroom, Uncle and Aunty in the other, three girls and me in one bedroom, and the boys out the back near the laundry. Not much room for personal space, and lots of physical contact all around.

I won't be a part of the fantasy that only trans people, or the freaks, have to engage a struggle of learning gender norms in childhood. Many, if not most of us, have experienced it at varying levels. Just like many FTMs, butches, femmes, and straight girls, I was indeed labeled a "tomboy" growing up. Relatives would come over and call me by my brother's name. My dress sense, my looks, my walk, and my attitude had already long caused my family to ask the question "What is wrong with you?" Time and time again I had embarrassed them, way before I ever knew what was going on.

You have to understand growing up in a Latin/Hispanic household there are a few things you don't muck around with, let alone question: God, Family, Food and Gender. In fact, this is so understood that there is not even a need to speak about any of it. It just is. Not necessarily in the above particular order, but these things are deadly serious, at least in my family it is and was, there's no romanticizing it. A man is a man. He works hard and plays even harder. He is strong, he is confident and he submits to no one (except God, his mother, and maybe his wife). A woman is a woman, she is weak yet strong, independent yet a born mother, she cooks well, she smells good, she works hard but it's woman's work, she has long hair and needs a man around, even if she thinks she doesn't. Both man and woman are family-oriented: both will have a deep desire to breed and carry on the family name and traditions. These were my taught gender norms, messages received 24/7 growing up.

I was as different then as I am now, perhaps more so. I know I felt a lot more like the odd one out with the initial (and continual) pressure from my parents. Pressure to not laugh so loud, or not sit the way I sat or play the way I played. The pressure to "act like a girl", but we can't all learn it, can we? Some just can't and some just won't. I guess that's part of what you have to expect from something that is learned and social – no social construct has a 100% success rate. While there are specific masculine and feminine characteristics, there is also a lot of conformity, role-play, and caricatures of what specific role-playing needs to be adhered to, depending on what's between your legs, regardless of what's between your ears and in your soul.

As I got older, perhaps 6, the pressure turned physical: I was spanked and held down, forced to put dresses on. My parents actually chased me and held me down to put ribbons in my hair. It was traumatic to me then, I cried like it was the end of the world. I cried and watched my brother pull faces at me and make fun of me – we both knew he had it good.

Today I can laugh. I mean, my poor parents just wanted me to look "beautiful", no? My mother had a daughter and that meant certain things, but her first and only daughter was none of these things. Of course, there was the constant fact that I was a humiliation to all the beautiful girls and women in our family. After all, that was what my family was known for and what my parents couldn't handle. They kept telling themselves and me was that I was beautiful and nice. I was so beautiful it was a sin not to put me in pink dresses and frilly socks, this was how it had to be!

In my own way, even though I didn't sit nice, I was nice. I was nice once, even kind of quiet and passive, but the constant pressure of not measuring up, and the physical and mental humiliation, changed me somewhat from being free and me to being secretive and being me, being a fighter and being me, being hidden but still me.

The other side to it, the side I know to be truest in my heart, is that I feel my parents gave to me so much more than they took. They gave me what has stuck with me, who I am apart from gender and sexuality, who I would be tomorrow if I was dumped in a third world country, who I would be if every commodity and the community I knew finished. Who I am and who I would be is a lot of what my parents wished me to be. I have enormous strength of character and belief in myself. Generations of my family on both sides have instilled the value of hard work, of family, of love. The contradictory values of "Be proud of who you are", " No one is better than you", "Stand up for yourself": they all stayed with me – gave me the strength to be able to today survive in the binary male/female world as something, somewhat othered.

When I started school here I spoke not a word of English. By year three, I was leader of the boys' gang and organizing kids older than me in sports, in fights, in card games they had never heard of. I never felt like I was impersonating a boy, if anything they were impersonating me and that was no feeling, that was a fact. Girls loved me and hoped to marry me. Teachers even as late as my first year of high school addressed my autograph book to "he." I was as dumb as they came in school. Girls did my homework for me, anyone that made fun of me I trampled – I became a bully, a victimizer before anyone could make me their victim. My guard was up 24/7. Yes, I was different but unlike the other different kids (the fairy boys, the spics/wogs, the fat, the ugly), I was unable to be infiltrated or brought down, I didn't cry and I wasn't beaten up. I became the best at everything that mattered, everything that was cool in my neighborhood, whether it was building a go-kart or playing soccer.

I am not proud of how I conducted myself during those years, how I unleashed all the pressure of being me, being different, being humiliated by my family and humiliating my family. I was carrying this secret, I thought, a secret that something was wrong with me. I was a Junior A grade soccer player, then at 13 I was not allowed to continue playing soccer on the boys' team. Playing on the girls' team was a humiliation to me: a betrayal and a sham! I had played on the boys' team since I was 6, I was the star player, how could they do this to me, was I not put on this earth to be the next Pele? No world-class champions played on girls' teams! Even the other boys fought to keep me on, not because they cared but because, like me, to them winning was everything and they didn't stand a chance without me. And what were these two fucking bumps growing on my chest anyway?

Of course I wished I were a boy, I had wanted boy things all my life. Boys were given the type of treatment, toys, clothes, and respect I needed. Boys were allowed to do what I wanted to do, but I was not. I remember an Aboriginal friend of mine telling me that when she was a kid she only wished she was white because she wanted what they had and to be treated better. Even as a young girl she was secretly proud to be black and never really wanted to be white. I really relate to that.

Had I been left to dress as I wanted, openly have a girlfriend at school, play the sport I wanted, and have the career I wanted, without pressure, harassment and violence — although I still became an auto mechanic regardless of my family's threats and social judgments — who knows if I'd still have wished I was a boy, or if it even would have crossed my mind? I may have chosen to transition into male, or I may have ended up a happy housewife in the suburbs, or possibly even… turned out exactly as I am today.

Now in my 30s, fluent in both English and Spanish, damage control in check, empowered with the knowledge of my Genderfusion, here I stand. Why do I choose to be referred to as "he" instead of "she"? A year ago next week I flew to the other side of the world and had "Top Surgery" (double mastectomy / chest reconstruction). Sounds strange but I wanted to be whole, I dreamed about it all my life; then a wonderful woman told me it was possible. I won't say I needed it as I could still live and function without it – in some ways it was pure indulgence. I don't want to upset anyone but it was not gender reassignment for me, though it was seeing myself on the outside how I do on the inside, like someone with a big nose that hates it and wants it off.

I don't want to offend or disrespect people who are trans (gender/man/woman/sexual). The trans part of transgender is more transient than transitioning. I am no more woman or man today than I was before the surgery. I still feel that same difference I felt when I was a child. Within me still exists my own gender: it may be a combination of both binary male and female or it may well be what I suspected all along, a gender unto itself – I don't know.

Today, left to my own devices out of my Saturn return and 20s, living in a world where I can make myself a man on the outside via hormones, surgery, birth certificate gender change, I ask myself of my childhood, *Did I wish I was a boy?* Or did society make me feel like I had to be a boy? Make me wish I were a boy by excluding me from what I was good at, what came naturally and what I wanted by trying to keep *their* toys, *their* sports, *their* clothes and *their* girls away from me?

Were the men afraid I wouldn't be accessible to them sexually, as a wife, as a mother? Were men afraid that I was better at *their* things and *they* would suffer humiliation at my hand? That *they* would lose out and I would force *them* into the kitchen and into a dress, and into netball and tennis? And then they would feel, they naturally would wish that they were a girl 'cause girls got the girls, girls were the sports stars, girls commanded 75% of everything, and girls were doing what they wished they could do.

Society applauds when women get breast implants, breast lifts. They are making their breasts look more like what the world tells them they should look like. Decisions may be socially charged via the media and patriarchal pressures on women, or it may simply be what the woman wants, or a combination of both. It all ranges from subliminal to overt but the societal gender influence is there.

Then I have to ask, why when someone chooses to cut their breasts off rather than pump them up, is it self-mutilation? Self-hatred? Mental illness? Gender reassignment? Is my choice cosmetic? I am choosing to make myself look more like I want to look, why if anything is it not seen as vanity? If my choice is in fact self-mutilation then so be it, but you can't pick and choose — liposuction, nose jobs, boob jobs, face peels, fake tans, back waxes, body piercing — you're all going down with me.

Why, if I cut them off, must I choose male? Why must it be gender reassignment? Why must I choose anything? "Top surgery", mastectomy, whatever you want to call it - I cut my breasts off. No therapy, no permission, no regrets, no sadness. Only joy, and a feeling of pure ecstasy, freedom and connectivity with my body that I had never felt before. Today I love my body and it feels right to me, it feels mine — a really weird thing for a person like me to say, believe me.

It would be so easy for me to live as a (trans) man. I fit society's ideals of what is male down to a "T". I am tough, physically strong, street smart, into hard sports, hard drink, gambling, and women, am a protector, destructor, dominating, self-assured. In all honesty I wouldn't have to change anything about myself, not even my name. Even if I weren't 100% with the decision but somewhere between 50 and 90%, it would still work out okay. I know that because I've lived thirty-some years as a "she" and it wasn't/ hasn't been any more than 20% right for me.

I never chose female and I won't choose male, both are untrue for me. It's like you have a dog and a cat, then you bring a little donkey home. You can't just make it be a dog or a cat 'cause it sort of looks a bit like either. Even if you put a diamonte collar on it, call it Lassie and make it beg, it's still a little donkey.

My decision not to choose male could be as socially charged as my childhood wish to be a male, before I understood what all the differences meant. Maybe society damaged me too hard and for too long? Maybe it's because my World Cup chance was taken away because my birth certificate said "Female" and that was the ONLY reason. Maybe it's all the physical and verbal bashings life has dished out upon me.

The pressure to choose is there, no doubt about that. Sometimes I feel like even my family subliminally pressures me without knowing what they are doing. My father has said to me, in Spanish, "Don't think your mother and I don't know that you were meant to be a boy." That said, if I were to transition to male they would bury me in the backyard; if they knew about the top surgery they would bury me in the backyard. A hard way to live? I don't know any other way.

My parents forbade me to be an auto mechanic, so when I became the first 'female' apprentice Mechanic of the Year, I attended the ceremony alone and watched all the other male nominees and their proud families. I did my entire four-year automotive apprenticeship without my parents' knowledge. They were long, hard, low-paying days, sometimes with no respect given to me in the workplace. This was 1989-92, not a passage from a '50s novel. I want to make it clear that not only don't I seek recognition as a male but I don't seek recognition as a female either. My recognition as a woman has come from being yelled at from strangers' cars, or being bashed by English backpackers in my own country, on my own street. My recognition as a "woman" comes from the wear and tear years of gender humiliation caused to my family. My recognition as a "woman" comes from the ending of a longterm lesbian relationship and the powerlessness in not having any say over the children I raised for years.

In all honesty the recognition I have received as a woman is all more than enough for me, I don't think I could deal with one smidgen more. But it is all a part of some experience, sentimentality and personality shaping that I can't turn my back on. In many ways society created me, made me so. They stomped on me and messed with me because I played great soccer, liked girls, and wouldn't wear a dress, because I was better at being a boy than most any of the other boys, and no one likes that, do they? Initially it may have been that simple, who'll ever know? Society virtually gagged and tied me to a fence to whip me into shape and this me is the shape I was whipped into.

So now here I am, the result of their whipping and messing with the nature God created. A transgendered, post op, tough as fuck, working in their world as a male, secretive, smart and shifty as the night falls, "gender outlaw" who has discovered his true self and is completely out of hand, even by my own standards.

So don't tell me I messed with what God created.

So I continue to wear the female and male traits like a skintight body suit and it makes me, me. All of the experiences have humbled me, broken and rebuilt me. Like the dog and the cat, the little donkey walks on all fours and shares common habits but is definitely a different species. Can't we just love donkeys as well and as much as dogs and cats?

Ultimately no doctor, theorist, fundamentalist, or lover has the right to determine whether I am male or female, whether other genders exist or I am simply imagining it. As I read somewhere once, "I think I'm too important to leave my fate up to anyone else." Reshaping who I am daily to my environ-ment forms who I am, right back to the days of wearing my shorts under my school uniform.

But now society has more reason to fear me than before, or perhaps a real reason. They should have left me alone from the beginning. Left me to fail (or succeed) of my own accord as a world-class soccer player. Left me to suffer embarrassment by my parents' gushing and public adoration at my apprentice of the year ceremony. Left me to have had a marriage and then a divorce from my wife, fighting it out in court as to who gets the kids – it all would've, I would've, been so ordinary, no? Isn't that what society wanted in the first place?

It's ironic, no? I'll lie my ass off to be what I really am, to survive honestly by being me – just like I have always had to. I won't be boxed in. I won't be forced to choose so others can be comfortable. I won't be the only one who is uncomfortable. This is just how it works for me.

If I Should Die Before I Wake... Don't Let Me
9/26–11/4/02   For Brotha Bear
Imani Henry

Black boys don't sleep.

They lie awake... dreaming bout what there could be

What's beyond these four walls?

Or lay up terrified by memories,

brain shattered

bone deep nightmares

pricking you like broken glass

recalling everything that was never said or done or was done and said too much

Black boys don't sleep.

They lie awake hoping there's choices ...somebody said something about choosing – what that got to do with me? – what choice do I have? — ain't got the luxury to be choosy!

Massa's house up on the hill, got big windows, lots of grass out front. He and Missy play their music loud, dancing in the window all carefree

They ain't eating scraps, they ain't fighting pigs for it, they ain't wearing burlap sacks, they ain't whipped cuz they is too tired, like us

… Black boys don't sleep.

We lie awake wondering what's beyond these four walls? What we missing out on? What happens when we be the last ones off the bus? When there's only white folks left. Do they let 'em on the bus for free? Do pretty women serve champagne while the band plays on?

'Til another one of us gets on and it all goes back to normal – we will never know - will we?

Black boys smile too much, too saucy, too uppity for their own good! Just cuz you got a little bit of education doesn't mean you be somebody! Know something!

Black boys be lazy, they should thank god for what we gives them, be grateful for what they get!

Ain't it good enuf for you, Boy?!

Black boys be tricky! Better watch 'em. Don't turn your back on none 'em. Never know what they gonna do!

Black boys be lying wait – plotting, pretending they is thinking. Planning –

counting backwards in their mind –

"Is this gonna be the day I kill 'em all? Is this gonna be the day?"

Black boys don't sleep. They sit up dreaming bout being president, astronaut, preacherman, doctor, knowing all the while, somebody's gonna hand them a broom and pail —

You miss a spot!

Knowing all the while someone's gonna ask them to

Put your back into it

Wash my car

Get this packet to Smith

STEP AWAY FROM THE CAR

KEEP YOUR HANDS WHERE I CAN SEE THEM

This is bigger than you.

You have no control.

There is nothing you can do

GET DOWN ON THE FLOOR!

What if I told you that it was safe now – you can come out and play?

We've slain all the dragons, rounded up all the king's men, drown them in the moat. The drawbridge is down and the castle is ours!

Would you come back? Would you come riding all shiny armored on a Black steed?

There is a princess AND a prince that needs rescuing in the tower. Would you come back?

What if I told you we've taken over the plantation?!

Got Massa and Missy at gunpoint, baking us biscuits in the kitchen — the table is set all pretty — got soft beds to sleep in — wearing fine silk and satin — plenty of food to eat now —

You can come on over. Would you come back?

What if I told there was another Black boy was born six days before you

–His name is Kwame –

means born on Saturday – (Saturday don't mean the same thing, no more) – But I know he is HE now, but I know his parents and I know his sister and he can be SHE anytime he wants to. Whenever he/she wants to. So will you come back? Would you come back?

What if I told you ain't nobody gonna follow you around no store no more. The streets are paved with gold – Ain't nobody homeless – And we're all living in mansions – Black people are treated with respect – Got Trans people walking round with dignity – There is justice in the WORLD!!!

O.K., I'm lying. But would you come back?

They tell me a friend is a terrible thing to waste.

Black boys don't sleep. I lie awake at 2:30 in the morning writing poems about other Black boys. Poems they will never read. And I curse, and scream, and cry.

And say Goddamn you!

Now how the hell I'm suppose to sleep.

I got shit to do in the morning, man.

How you gonna up and leave me?

You see they got us surrounded

You see they got us outmanned, out-gunned!

We need every solider, damn it, every solider.

Did all that Training to be part of this special elite armed force.

This special operation unit fighting on all fronts, BROTHA!

I know you were tired.

You said you were tired, and I hear you, cuz we all gets tired.

But that's why we used just duck out for a minute,

Stop listening to the gunfire, find ourselves some a shady tree.

Take off the pack back, and CONVERSATE – in code –

in language they don't speak.

Talk bout first facial hair,

Sending out femmes undercover to buy binders in the lingerie store. Talk about midwest vs. east coast vs. lesbians vs. gay boys, talk about god vs. Marx

talk about anything... cuz

 how many people say they've been a Black woman and a Black man in the same lifetime

...so please let's talk about anything, cuz dead folks can't talk about shit!

Black boys don't sleep. They lie awake at 4:53 a.m. Looking at these four walls, writing an epic poem for another Black boy, who no longer can read. Thinking bout 5 hours, over beer in a hotel room in August – and it doesn't matter what we said anymore —

Did I tell him, "I love you, man" ...

Did he hear me? Did he?

He couldn't… hear us – any of us.

And all my ranting and raving and our crying and cursing – Won't bring him back. He ain't coming back.

But there are other Black boys that ain't sleeping neither.

They're wide awake, pacing like panthers, and they get tired too. So we got find us some more trees for them soldiers to duck behind. Find us some shade far from the firing line.

Gotta say "You look tired, Brotha, I can see in your eyes.

We ain't letting you fight without no sleep, & there ain't no compromise."

So until you ready, I got your back.

Gotta say, "Til you ready we'll keep watch. It may look like there is only six of us now, but I KNOW we got a whole army coming."

And some us of are living and some us ain't , but we ALL gonna keep watch over you.

So you sleep, Black boy, go to sleep

And We'll wake you

when it's time,

to rise and

to fight again.

Disclosure
Daniel Ray Soltis

I went to a women's college. These days when I tell people that I usually add a laugh or at least an amused shrug. Kind of ironic, isn't it, now that I am identifying and—as much as possible—living as a man, that I spent four years of my life in an environment where the one nonnegotiable criterion for belonging was claiming (and if necessary proving) one's identity as a woman? I wonder, as I continue this process called transition, if I will reach a point—perhaps after my license has its little M—when I won't know how to tell people that. What will I put on my resumé?

"It says here you went to Bryn Mawr," the interviewer will say, peering at the bespectacled young man in a suit and goatee. "Isn't that all women?" He'll smile and spread his hands.

"It's a long story..."

What will I tell new acquaintances? Will I go into detail after they ask what they thought was a simple question? Will I just state the facts and leave it up to confusion? Will I switch my memories to the coed college a mile down the road? Will I simply erase four years of my life?

What will it mean if I am willing to erase parts of my life in order to successfully "pass"? Am I that afraid of judgement? That ashamed of who I am? I went to a women's college—in large part *because* it was a women's college. I hoped to meet women who I could identify with, who were smart and serious and probably a little weird. I wanted to learn what it could mean to grow up in this gender I thought was an unchangeable given. I did. I learned my politics there. I learned to be a feminist and a radical and an activist. I learned what confident women's camaraderie feels like. I had my first sexual experiences with *other* women, learned math and physics (and what it feels like to be a woman in a male-dominated field), how to be economically self sufficient. I worked on a feminist newspaper and started drawing comics about being queer and female. I got a women's symbol tattooed on my arm, embroidered "Lesbian" onto my backpack.

How could I gender-neutralize those years and still have a story with any authenticity? How could I erase them and still be myself with any authenticity?

And yet, here I am, contemplating it.

At True Spirit this year, the organizers are planning on checking legal IDs, so they can weed out the minors and restrict their access to the more overtly sexual workshops. In addition, some minors were given a form to fill out that includes legal name, parental permission, and some health information. In addition to anger about discrimination and restricting the access of minors to places and events that could, on some level, save their lives (never mind an assumption that these minors can and should be out enough to their parents to get permission to attend a trans conference), people are upset about the sheer indignity of it—how many 17-year-olds have changed their legal names to match their chosen names? For some, this may be the only place where they can be fully out and accepted as male, and yet they are forced to bring along the baggage of their female name, have it scrutinized, known.

It's common courtesy in the FTM community not to ask for female names—for female pasts—unless someone volunteers the information. This "he" thing can be so nebulous; sometimes a space is safe only because you know the female appellations aren't there for people to default into.

To deny or ignore female birth can be to erase the past. To claim it loudly and openly can be to erase the present. I will never be "just a guy," but I certainly demand to be seen and treated as a guy. How do I claim my complexity without losing my present validity? I am FTM because I am seeking to be whole. Yet "successfully transitioning" can often imply cutting off large portions of one's past. Who will I be in five years? How will I really be whole?

My Gender Tale
Cj Gross

When I was growing up, it was easy to be a tomboy. I lived in the woods and played in the woods, and lots of other girls also wore clothing that might seem appropriate for your average tomboy. I didn't feel like a girl though but it didn't bother me because I didn't have a family that pushed me to be more feminine in any way. I just noticed it. I spent a lot of time alone in the woods and there were definitely times, many times, when I felt like I was really a boy. I just kind of knew that I was something other than a girl. I didn't talk to anyone about it, because I had such a rich private world, which included lots of time in the woods. It just seemed like another one of those private things about me that no one would understand anyway.

When I was about sixteen (I was already living alone by then) I would tape my very small tits down with duct tape (do not try this at home), stuff a sock into my pants, and look in the mirror. I did this quite often. I would admire myself and just wonder what my body would feel like if it truly existed like the image I admired in the mirror. It did not feel like a sexual thing, and I really didn't think about it much. This was a private thing I did and it didn't upset me; it was just something I enjoyed.

In my early twenties I was doing a lot of Reevaluation Counseling (a kind of peer counseling). I was encouraged to lead a support group for women. I had a lot of resistance to doing this but eventually decided to try it. Mostly I ended up talking about how the identity "woman" didn't fit for me and felt extremely limiting. It was actually the first time I had spoken to anyone about this and I could tell that it made people uncomfortable. Although I knew others in the group felt sorry for me and thought I wasn't embracing my womanhood, I still kept talking about my feelings. I didn't feel bad about it really. I figured they just didn't understand.

I remember being with a girlfriend and noticing a dress in a store window. She practically pushed me into the store, telling me I would look so great in this dress. So I reluctantly tried it on and she was right, it looked really good and very sexy. At the time there was no way I would ever buy a dress like that, so I laughed and left the store. Over the next couple of weeks I visited that store and tried the dress on about five times. I said to myself, "If I were a guy, I would buy this in a second and wear it for drag." Then I decided to buy it, because I didn't want my biological gender to stop me from having it.

In my mid-to-late twenties I started to think about a sex change. I wanted more of my boy out in the world. I was tired of being private and it didn't feel right since it was bothering me more and more. I looked into the possibility of a sex change, but realized that it wouldn't work for me, because I didn't feel particularly male either. Besides that, the surgery and hormones scared me too much. I had moved to San Francisco where it seemed there were so many identities to choose from and I began feeling very confused. Part of my confusion was that I didn't look or act really butch so I felt lost and started to question this boy place (or place that didn't feel female) and doubt myself. I felt like I didn't fit in with the transgender community or the women's community either. I went through a time when I dressed more butch, but that didn't seem to solve anything within what was becoming a stronger and stronger discomfort with my gender(s).

A few years later I started doing S/M and felt there was a context where I could explore very deep and real places in me, places that I had never been public about. I felt so validated, incredibly fulfilled, and happy to be acknowledged and taken seriously. It was finally understood by some other people within that setting that this was not about role playing. There were different places inside that simply did not fit into any gender identity easily, or at all. There were also places that were very male which I could finally be out about. Finally, I was not alone.

The last couple of years I have started to enjoy dressing more feminine sometimes. I still feel the same, neither female nor male. I just don't care so much what others see. People who really get to know me will find out soon enough.

I have been getting more involved with the transgender community, and it is bringing up a lot of complicated feelings. I want the trans community to stretch and welcome people like myself that may not look so androgynous (though I can if I work at it) but feel androgynous. I want people of all kinds to be welcome, even if they don't feel they fit into the current gender system. It's a big stretch and I know people have a lot of different feelings about it. Even within the genderqueer community I feel I am in the minority because I pass as female and so there are a lot of things I have not had to deal with. On the other hand, I constantly have to deal with assumptions about who I am. I also have to explain why I am at transgender meetings. I must explain that I am not only an ally because I am not simply female. There is no place I feel I nicely fit and I hope that the transgender community will welcome me. I like to think of myself as multi-gendered or genderfluid, as Kate Bornstein says. I love knowing now that I am not alone.

Your Used Eyelashes
Blake Nemec

I'd seen John before and remembered he loves listening to girls' office talk. He wanted to be one of the girls, and he came to me to wear his girl skin. So I got into my butch daddy skin and dragged his face over the carpet of the dungeon floor. He didn't like it and would prematurely cut into a whiny, slutty girl role. I did tell him I would give him a gender transformation, and soon he would become a girl. He was paying me a straight day's wage for one hour of my time, but his misogynistic choice of girl was boring. Besides, it was too early in our session for him to transition. My butch daddy role was equally tired, but in a 5' 2", 130 lb. body, it was the only male gender the tricks would take seriously.

In my pro-domme scenes, and in my life, I wanted to express both genders. In that scene, I expressed the femme when John did. Once I bound John up with a Japanese rope dress. I electrocuted his cock and balls and slapped him around a bit. After a half-hour of domming him as a male, I would let him explore the female gender. I would dress him up as a woman, listen to his responses of the gender play, then throw him into a rehearsal scene for the "Cabaret". I liked to push the roles of Xena, Judge Judy, Joan Jett, and Diamanda Galas. It gave him a good challenge. Depending on the submissive, and their understanding of the complexities of the female gender, I could debase or applaud their efforts.

Mid-session, I left the dungeon and strutted down a flight of carpeted stairs to the pros' locker room. I was almost naked by the time I got to my locker and had my Ace binder, wifebeater t-shirt, leather pants, and biker boots fallin' out of my arms because I only had an hour. Out came my turquoise three-inch Steve Madden heels with the '80s side zipper, an elastic silver tube sock dress, and my blue disco wig. Into the bathroom where I wrestled into nylons, garter belt and bra, then fumbled to get the other clothes onto my body. I stretched my eyes to the side to create a flat pallet for eyeliner, then smeared blue glitter shadow over my eyes and mahogany lipstick, like dried tomato paste, over my lips. It was all there, up to eyebrows that soared into my hairline. I was the Sisters of Perpetual Indulgence's trailer child.

I began to strut out of the locker room when Terri, who reminded me of a straight Aileen Wuornos, says, "Rogue, you look so cute as a femme, you really should switch!"

I walked out of the kitchen in short straight steps, clutching a glass of water like it would help my balance, and gave Terri a blank look, saying, "This is drag, Terri. Fun, but not a perfect fit."

She'd reply, "No, really. You're really pretty."

"Well, off to my little lesbian," I said, sighing through the words.

She scrunched her eyebrows, and shook her head saying, "AdOHHrable."

Terri is in the same kitchen as my father and brothers. Pigs in a blanket cheering for Velveeta cheese, a nice little American treat. Happy for a familiar glob of useless starch to sit and rot in the stomach. Once it manages to roll into the ass it will only be shat out. Those who cheered for the cute American plate will ask what happened, it was so cute and tasty before.

I never wanted to be shat out. I wanted to drive into bloodstreams. I walked up the stairs to find John cuddled in a rope web, exactly as I instructed. I began, "Liza, you poor thing, let me help you out of those rags. You've only got five minutes until showtime, and no one forgets a debut."

I went through the dress-up routine I just had with myself, but this time helping "Liza". I enjoyed the similarities of our bodies: hairy legs, roly-poly stomach, underarm hair, short disheveled haircut, and ugly feet. I also enjoyed sewing in a '70s sisterhood dynamic with the men who wanted to explore the female gender, so I did that part of the scene as a queen. I let "Liza" walk behind me, my hips and ass against her hips and crotch, teaching her how to sway her hips. We role-played that she would be performing her own music for the first time. She would sing a song called "Effervescent Eyelash," that went like this:

I know your boa from backstage
I smoke your butts when you leave
but what I love
what I love most
your used lashes

In that scene, John was a janitor for a drag club. He/she fantasized about being on stage and after years of janitorial service, the management found her in after-hours drag. She pleaded for some stage time and they gave her a Monday night slot.

"Liza" lurched across the room all shoulders and legs while her long hairy arms jutted into the room's sky and it was beautiful. I clapped and cheered for her sincerely. She stared into the room's mirror, breathing deeply, breathing slowly. We hugged like teenage girls, and I did everything to make her feel accepted and box-less. I told her she was a star. Then I told her to get on stage, or in that case, to the shower.

After I escorted John out of the House of Ill Repute, I went back to the locker room, this time for myself. In the shower I washed off my make-up and the other drag personages, and looked forward to a kinky sweaty night at the Cud Club, where the dance floor crowd would applaud my own gender expression by convulsively dancing with me. I also thought about money. I hoped I would be able to turn three more of those tricks in the next week to pay rent.

My other part-time job as a personal attendant only put a bit more than a hundred dollars every couple of weeks in my pocket. Being a professional submissive opposite being a pro-domme was interesting. I was an emergency attendant and assisted 20 or so different disabled people in the course of a month. I never knew who would call for assistance on my shift, and with each month new clients arrived while others left. So I didn't go into pronouns with people I might only see that night. My trans identity in that world was invisible.

I went back to my locker and got out an old iron-on "Philly's Catch It" shirt, black jeans, ACE bandage, old skool Adidas sneakers, and boxer briefs. I bound my rocks in a sock, and slowly slid the clothes on; I pomaded my head, took my cut of cash, walked out the door, and rode off on my bicycle. En route to the city, I rode into King's liquor store, picked up a bottle of Canadian Mist and hopped on the old Chimo road bike when some dude came up to me and said, "Hey, man, can you spare some change?"

I just shook my head no.

"Hey... ma'am?" he said while he started to walk beside me. I remained silent starting to roll away.

"Hey, what are you? Say something. HEY! HEY!" With the last hey, he grabbed my shoulder and yanked me off my bike. It took me a body's length of space to fall off so I took that distance between us and scooted back on the road bike and took off, physically untouched. My bike felt flimsy and I feared the mere aluminum and rubber couldn't get me out of there. Just like I feared my rubbery identity, my ability to pay bills and evolve, was going to snap back into the pavement instead of moving forward. But there are chains, cables, and grease to a bike. There's bone, blood, and back to a body. I did catch speed, found air to run through my blood to my back, and bone to drive my legs.

Punk Rock Carnival Whores: A Story
Martin Inane

The San Francisco Transgender Film Fest had just ended. My roommate and I threw a party at our apartment in the East Bay. It was supposed to be a sex party, but only a few people actually had sex. Most people were hanging out in the living room, drinking and listening to Siouxsie and the Banshees. A carload of people materialized; they'd just come from Let's Get Fucked Up, a party at the Odeon. Someone was making prank calls: "We're from the homo militia. We're coming for your children. What we don't fuck, we eat!

I noticed a thin guy in a beige beret who was sitting in a corner. Flanking him were two attractive, androgynous punks... One had curly black hair, wore oversized Lolita sunglasses, a tight skirt, and fishnets. The other had bleached hair, bright red lipstick, and wore a bomber jacket. She looked like a drag queen. When I heard her speak, I knew this was not the case. No drag queen in his wildest fantasy could have produced such a squeaky voice. It turned out that she was the singer for a thrash-metal band.

"Hey," my roommate said to me. "There's some people in the hot tub."

The tub was outdoors, and was shared by the apartment complex.

"Uh, it's locked at night," I protested. I walked outside and saw a gaggle of queers squeezed into the sauna. They'd jumped a big fence and were reclining au natural. At one point, a suburban passerby received the education of his life when he witnessed the array of punk fags, dykes, and trannies in all their body-mod glory hovering around the hot tub!

The guy in the beret came over and started talking to me. He was soft-spoken and seemed to be moderately intelligent. I admired the tattoos on his arms. I didn't feel compelled to be conversational. He noticed the tribal design on my shoulder, and lifted my arm to peer at it.

"Are you a Taurus?" he inquired. I grimaced.

Oh no, I thought. Please don't engage me in conversation about horoscopes. I get enough of that already.

"No, I was in Spain. It was my first tattoo, and I wanted a bull." I explained.

"It looks good," he smiled seductively. "My name's Justin by the way." As it happened, he had some travelling experiences himself. He mentioned touring with Nine Inch Nails as the member of a popular alternative circus troupe.

"You were in a circus?" I asked, interested.

"Yeah, I was the Rubber Man. You know, the contortionist." He brushed a strand of floppy, pretty-boy hair away from his face. He talked about his friendship with Chicken John, ex-bandmate of G.G. Allin and progenitor of the Odeon Bar: San Francisco's watering hole for carnival folk. That's when I really started looking at him and paying attention. Nothing turns me on like carnie folk. I remembered reading about Chicken John's punk rock circus in

Maximum Rock'n'Roll and fantasizing about joining the troupe one day. To be an exhibitionist! To live on the road! It sounded like heaven to me. When would they come to *my* town?

At some point in the evening, I found myself in a bedroom with him. He and a porn-star friend were groping each other. The ensuing sexcapade lasted until about six in the morning. I was surprised to hear from him a few days later. He was doing work on a house near Lake Merritt. Having retired from his circus career, he was now employed as a home renovator. I told him I'd be right over in an hour, and soon found myself in the home of an eccentric, new-age yuppie woman. It was like a house from a Daphne DuMaurier novel: every room had its own character, albeit of the creepy and unoccupied variety. The living room was oriental tapestries, tasseled pillows, expensive minimalist furniture.

"Look at the French doors," Justin was saying. He ushered me from room to room like a proud curator in a museum of the neurotic. On the second floor was a bedroom with clouds painted on the ceiling. Justin was tense as he pondered how to integrate the room with its furnishings appropriately. "This room is like a puzzle," he said, rubbing his chin. We retired to the entertainment room. Debauchery seemed appropriate since we were surrounded by extravagant pieces of stereo and home theatre technology. I shivered at the decadence before me.

They were gaudy, and they were baubles. My obsessions seemed almost noble by comparison. Justin distracted me with a kiss. I don't know how to kiss, so I reached for his zipper. I felt up his chest. He had those extra-sensitive, small nipples. They reminded me of something a guy had said to me once, I have a penis between my legs, and two clitorises on my chest. While we were making out, he bent his arm backwards so that it seemed to disappear. We were a couple of freaks. We were fondling each other in a house that was spiritually inspired by the Rococo period.

I guess it made sense.

The next day, it was around one in the afternoon, and I was lying on top of Justin. He swatted my ass.

"Something has to happen, and it has to happen now," he stated matter-of-factly.

This was his way of saying that we should get our dazed, sex-saturated bodies out of bed. In a few days, he would fly back home to Boise, Idaho. If we'd been in a story by Petronius, we'd have stayed and lazed around in that mansion of decadence indefinitely. A rich old monarch telling obscene anecdotes over a dinner of roasted pig would have completed the image.

Fresh Cut of Divine
Westley Rutter

I run my fingers over her hair
playing with a section
starkly contrasting with my skin
pale enough to fade into the blank gray pressing on the
    window
Car windows smeared with fingerprints
hasty motions
Tea tree oil burns my lips
Swollen with kisses
Tinny speakers are singing meaningless
lyrics tied to memories still vivid
I'm ten again.
Sitting in a front seat too big with dog hair
broken heat in a cold November night
My dad beside me
The warmth of a pizza box on my lap
Listening to those songs I grew up with.
Old Cars' songs
and here I am staring out at trees ticking by.

Keeping time.
I wish I could still
speak to him.
That he could see I've grown up
a lot like him.
Father and son.
I think of how he would like this girl in my lap.
If he would only meet her.
She turns over. Drifting in and out of sleep.
I keep watching out filtered
glass. Watching the trees, marking the miles.
He stands awkwardly.
Wrapping the towel tightly around his waist.
Hazy morning
light blurring with bathroom glare on mirrors.
Still fogging his image.
He thinks how he looks best in low light reflection on glass.
For a minute he can look.
His body perfected in the mutilation
of the shower's glaze.
Raises a finger to the mirror.
Tracing the letters.
W-E-S.
His name.
In the letters are slivers of his face.
His skin. His flushed cheeks.
Pools forming at the points of the W.
 Dripping off the legs of the E
 sliding down the curves of the S.
His name cries.
Crying all down his reflection.
Messy like these days seem to be.
His hand smears it all away.

Eyes retreating from the body's reality. This is why they call him "she." He pulls the neoprene fabric around his torso. So tight across his chest. Wincing with the sting that erases the breast. With each tug he's closer and closer to that make or break pronoun. That recognition of self. With each tug he's marking off the days. The days until the mind of Wes and the body of Wes can meet. I clasp pens like weapons, fingering loose-leaf dreams. Hands nervous and blunt, slight in size and strong in theory. In notebooks stuffed with disorganization I pull out impersonal sheets. Photocopied in black and white. Assumptions that we will all fall in line. Black and white. But like this sweatshirt my arms retreat into, I'm awfully gray. I try to write my name down but it's too hard. I yearn for the first letter, a "W", but I regretfully write the C of my legal name. The name I can't fight within these walls of kids shouting mixed messages. Because sometimes I'm not afraid, but every face that's seen me all these years. Every face cuts the cords that hold the new identity up. All these years have piled on top of a scared little boy in a stretched-out sweater and scruffy hair. Those walls of kids keep testing me. Hands shoved deep in pockets. And wouldn't it be simpler? The teacher, he calls out a name that is vaguely associated with the painted girl on my body, slowly chipping away. They all see those paint chips. Gaudy colors, shaky lines. Guess they didn't catch on. I am watching the minute hand of that clock. And with each five minute mark I come closer. To getting out from these walls. Pouring paint remover all down my skin. Looking in the mirror, outside to in. Clothes worn thin with the blows. Soaked with tears over girls and a father and a body. Vision blurring. I am ticking off the minutes. I am tugging at the binder. I am marking off the miles. I am waiting. Waiting for my time.

Neither Stone Nor Wing
Eli Clare

SCARS

I pour a bath, dissolve a handful of mineral salts, catching each crystal in the stream of hot hot water, crack the window, try to light the candles. They float in a bowl of water, and as I touch match to wick, my hand jumps, tremor climbing the ladder of my arm. I swamp one candle, then the other, give up. Strip my clothes—flannel shirt, t-shirt, undershirt, Converse high tops threaded with purple laces, jeans, boxers. Pull off my binder, breasts coming free. I think about the not-so-long-ago laws against crossdressing, about old-time butches and the price they paid. The stories of bar raids, strip searches, and jail cells scare me.

Body buoyant, the heat stings, right arm loosening. Tremors rock water, no longer locked in shoulder and back. I finger the appendectomy scar that stretches almost all the way from my navel to my pubic hair, a thick, ropy trail the surgeon cut along the center. I cup the knobby glob of tissue on my right knee, the remnants of one fall among thousands. Trace the ridged line across my left palm, mark of a chisel slipping hard from wood to flesh.

My scars, except for the braid down my belly, don't come from a surgeon's knife, an unusual circumstance for anyone like me, physically disabled at birth or soon after. My quad muscles were never cut, sewn back together. Achilles tendons never severed. Legs, never broken, stretched slowly. Pins never inserted into hips and knees. I know many disabled people whose bodies are crisscrossed with scars, their childhoods punctuated by surgery. But not mine.

Nor do any of my scars come from all the years of rape and torture I lived through. I can't show you the knife slipping into vagina, the rope wrapping around wrist and ankle, the fire-red brand pushing between shoulderblades. My skin did not become a map. For that, I need to go subterranean. Muscles knotted, tendons inflamed, vertebrae too sore to touch: these are the scars I carry.

As I soak, the wind picks up outside, tosses the cedars and firs into a whispery dance, blows through the open window, then dies, leaving the night to a chorus of frogs. I submerge myself, tremor dissolved into hot water. Place a hand on the flat of my chest just above my breasts. One day I may have scars to trace here. Not the matted tissue of a radical mastectomy, hoping against hope the cancer won't return, but the feathery lines of a chest reconstructed to follow the ridge of pectoral muscle, surgery gladly chosen. Sometimes this is what I want, the curve of breast irrevocably gone. But will I let the doctors, scalpels in hand, touch my skin? Will I have enough desire, enough courage, enough money?

A dream: I lie on top of him, my left leg pressed between his, can feel his cock bulging there against my thigh. We have taken off only our shoes. Kissing slow, talking slow, I want to slide my hands up under his shirt, up to rest along his shoulderblades. Turn him over, his body arching into my weight, cup his balls in one hand, and take him gentle. I want to but don't. Instead we are kissing with all our clothes between us. I tell him, "If you want to be lovers with me, you need to know. On the streets we will be faggots, and in bed we will not forget."

Underwater I touch the bottom of the tub, white porcelain. Touch my skin, the tree frogs tattooed on my left leg—the first orange and black climbing off my ankle, the second green with red toes sitting mid-calf, the third yellow and black striped leaping toward my knee. When people ask about these tattoos, why I chose frogs, I say, "I dreamed them in vivid living color, and the dream wouldn't leave me alone." Touch myself, soft and warm. None of my scars come from a cop's billy club.

AMBIGUITY

I'm standing in the women's restroom at work, washing my hands. In my peripheral vision, I notice a woman walk in, look at me, walk back out. I know she's checking the sign on the door.

She returns, says to me, "You know this is the women's room," smiles. I say, "I know." She seems content.

A bright early autumn day, leaves just beginning to turn, I walk home from the food co-op, a car full of young men speed by. They yell, "Hey faggot," that word suddenly full of venom. Without thinking I flip them off, shout obscenities after their car. The homophobes never call me dyke. Either they don't know the word or don't recognize that I could be a woman.

I'm whitewater rafting on the Yough River with a bunch of my dyke friends, part of a large guided tour. We've spent all day on the river, navigating rapids, falling out of our boats, getting into water fights, cracking endless jokes. On the shuttle back, I sit by a middle-aged white guy. We talk about rivers, about rafting and canoeing. He asks, "Did you learn to canoe in the Boy Scouts?" I just shake my head, smile at his assumption, don't correct him. How would I explain my childhood collection of *Boys' Life*, my yearning to be an Eagle Scout, to learn orienteering and map-making, my one dismal attempt at being a Girl Scout?

I'm walking my dog and a friend's dog back from the park where we have spent the last half-hour playing catch. I now have them both on leash again, hands full, trying to hang onto two excited dogs and their spit-covered frisbee. A woman stops me. She wants to pet them, know their names. Then asks, "You a boy?" I say, "Nope," to which she replies, "You a girl?" looking truly puzzled. I leave quickly. There is no short answer.

CLOTHES

Mary Chapin cranked on the stereo. I dress to go out, singing along:

> *In this world you've a soul for a compass*
> *And a heart for a pair of wings*
> *There's a star on the far horizon*
> *Rising bright in an azure sky*
> *For the rest of the time you're given*
> *Why walk when you can fly?*

From the closet, I pull my black twill trousers, pleated and creased, a white dress shirt, the burgundy tie traced with black lines that a friend gave me months ago, a narrow black belt with gold buckle, and the blazer I bought a decade ago for a dollar. I start with a clean undershirt, wrap my breasts tight against my chest.

I am in the middle of a love affair with ties. I find myself at the mall, ostensibly shopping for sheets or towels, but really

I'm there just to check out the ties, touch the cacophony of silk patterns, the bright fans displayed in the windows of Hudson's, Nordstrom's, the Men's Warehouse. Find myself in the jumbled chaos of secondhand stores, searching for the narrowest of narrow black ties, textured with thin diagonal lines. A serious love affair.

I finish buttoning my shirt. Slip the burgundy tie under my collar, cross the two ends, pulling the wide one up and over, through the second loop. Draw the knot close to my neck, leave a dimple, exactly right. I adore how I look after I've shrugged into my blazer, put on my dress shoes, tie lying flat and smooth against my shirt, curve of breast and hip vanishing under my clothes.

Dream: Greyhound bus station, women's washroom. I look at myself in the mirror, notice that I am growing a beard, golden hair curling against skin. Pull my hands through the sunlight, happy but puzzled, because I know I have not yet started taking testosterone.

For most of my life I have hated clothes and hated shopping for them even more. I remember the trips. My mother and I drive the family's beat-up VW van 65 miles to the nearest shopping mall. She sets the agenda. First to the fabric store where she leafs through pattern books, pointing to the line drawings, asking, "Do you like this? What about that?" Asking, as if I care. How to choose between one ugly dress and another? I simply try to avoid lace and ruffles. Then we look for cloth, my mother sorting through the bolts to find just the right fabric at just the right price. She has no love affair with—or talent for—sewing. Rather, this is a strategy to save money, to clothe me and my siblings on a budget already stretched thin. After the fabric store, we go to Penney's to buy socks and underwear. I always make a beeline to the boys department to look at the flannel shirts, finger the stiff denim jeans, my mother tracking me down, leading me to the girls' racks.

Later when I had money of my own, I bought jeans and t-shirts which I wore to rags, the baggier the better. Clothes were to hide in, to tent over my body. I wanted no one to look at me, to call me pretty. Now as I begin to inhabit my body, pulling into this house made of skin and bone, muscle and tendon, after decades of absence, I have also started to like clothes, to lust after tuxedo jackets and black, rayon-backed vests, crisp oxford shirts and silver tie tacks. Started to pay attention to how I like my jeans to fit, baggy off the hip, how I like my flannel shirts to weather buttery soft. There are days now when I want to tuck my shirt in, wear a wide leather belt, and polish my boots. I want the girls to notice; the boys to flirt.

LANGUAGE

At the bar, dykes smile and nod my way, connecting butch to butch. Gay men cruise me hard, then look away. The bouncer cards me, surprised when I'm not a 15-year-old boy. The bartender calls me "cripple" and "girl" in a single glance.

In another world at another time, I would have grown up neither boy nor girl, but something entirely different. In English there are no words. All the language we have created—transgender, transsexual, drag queen, drag king, stone butch, high femme, nellie, fairy, bulldyke, he-she, FTM, MTF—places us in relationship to masculine or feminine, between the two, combining the two, moving from one to the other. I yearn for an image to describe my gendered self, not the shadow land of neither boy nor girl, a suspension bridge tethered between negatives. Rather I want a solid ground with bedrock of its own, wish for language to take me to a brand new place neither masculine nor feminine, day nor night, muscle nor bone, stone nor wing.

Dream: He comes to me as I last saw him just after his chest surgery, stands at the foot of my bed, chest sloping flat and broad into belly, belly hanging against belt. He fills his skin to its very edge as he never did when he was a woman, even a big butch dyke on her motorcycle. Soon he will have a beard. He says nothing; we just look at each other. Then I am alone, genitals changed—clit grown, not a penis nor the hooded fiddlehead of my female body, I have testicles nestled against me.

STONE

Floating down a glacier-carved river, water roiling around boulders big as boxcars, the banks lined with rock, worn smooth, warmed to the sun, I tell my friends, "In my next life, I want to be a stone, a rock face sloped into the current, a boulder at the lip." We all laugh. I sift sand and gravel through my fingers.

My father and his buddies did the unthinkable, unspeakable, unbidden. Some nights they tied me down, spread my legs wide. Some nights carved into me, electric shock jolting all the way down to bone. Some nights took fire to my skin. Some nights locked me in a cage and left me to the cold. Some nights hung me from a rafter in the barn. Often, my body shattered, this torture I've learned to call ritual abuse breaking me open. But there were also nights—hour heaped upon hour, tendon and muscle contracting against contraction—that turned my body to stone. I would reach deep into the quiet, my body and I. Settle beneath breath and pain and sound, beneath bone and blood into the quietest of quiet. My stone body. Stone. Untouched and untouchable. But inside lies another stone called pain. It has put me to bed at night, woken me up in the morning, knocked me to the ground. Pain is my stone body softening. And inside pain lives yet another stone, a geode cracked to amethyst.

Body of stone: let me respectfully leave you behind. And as

for pain, the aches and bruises, knots and splinters, ruptures and breaks, I can only hope that one day I will be done with you. But the geode broken open to its hollow-skinned center, mountain range of crystal—pink, lavender, midnight purple—yielding its strength but not giving way: in this stone I want to make home.

Dream: I take the weight of your breasts into both hands, watch your eyes close. We kiss deep, then deeper as dusk rises round us. Tongue and tooth, skin and muscle, I cover your body with mine, rock against your hips, gladly riding wide open into you. And when you reach toward me, I no longer flinch but want only the briefest of touch, winding my hands through your hair.

A river at dusk, its skin smooth and unbroken, sun no longer braided into sparkles. Cliff divers hurl their bodies from thirty, forty, fifty feet, bodies neither flying nor earthbound, three somersaults and a half turn, entering the water free-fall without a ripple: I live here. Stone and geode, butch and faggot, locked with tremor and scar, girl and boy and neither by turn, this body of mine.

Approaching Thirty:
Some Reflections on Survival and Activism
Joshua Mira Goldberg

In one month I'll be thirty years old. To my surprise, this birthday is a big deal to me. Part of the reason that this birthday is a big deal is that I never thought I'd actually make it to thirty. It seemed reasonable, looking at the way I was living my life in my teens and early twenties, to predict that I wouldn't make it to thirty. Many of my peers (trans and otherwise) never did make it this far, having died of suicide, overdose, murder, illness, or bad luck.

My survival is in large part due to the unrelenting and varied support of family, a few close friends, and many elements of luck. Being born into a family that fiercely advocated for me and into a society where I have had the privileges of being white and having access to some of the markers that determine class status. I'm sure that if I had had brown skin, or my family was perceived as being poor or uneducated, many of the service providers who intervened at various points in my life would have written me off as a hopeless case, or been quicker to force treatments on me that would have rendered me even more fucked up than I already was.

My own lurch of survival mirrors, in many ways, the tenuous survival of my family and my cultural community. Four generations ago, my family fled from shtetls (rural villages) in Eastern Europe and Russia to urban centers in America and Canada. All the members of my community are alive because they or their family members were able to flee pogroms and/or the Shoah (Holocaust). My family members survived, while their siblings, neighbors, parents, and children perished from the hunger, exposure, brutality, and despair.

My family has a tremendously strong knack for survival, but there have also been casualties: at least one person dead by suicide, others struggling with substance use and abusive relationships, one woman left permanently disabled by electroshock therapy. In my chosen families of trans/genderqueer and activist communities, many people of my generation are reeling from the effects of sexual and physical violence, on the brink of poverty, and struggling to cope with persistent mental and physical illness.

At times the weight of the many who didn't survive is terribly overwhelming. There is so much suffering among the dead, people whose lives were ended early because of injustice, that the ongoing suffering experienced by the majority of the world feels unbearable. At other times, the trail of ghosts seems to prop me up, helping to keep me moving along even when I am wracked with self-pity and despair. My great-grandparents didn't walk from Russia to Western Europe in isolation. They survived as part of a community of refugees, all walking towards to the same boat to take them to the country they believed would be a deliverance from oppression (not realizing their arrival would contribute to putting the indigenous people of this land in the same situation they were fleeing from).

Each lurch I take towards survival is taken with the love and support of many others struggling to move not only themselves but the whole world in that direction. The miracle of our communal survival leaves me feeling so grateful to so many beings—all my ancestors, my extended family, my communities, my friends, the plants and animals and water and other elements that have made my physical survival possible—this is a tremendous amount of support. And responsibility.

I think of Jewish liberation as being more than just fighting anti-Semitism—instead I feel it to be intimately connected to land issues, colonialism, and cultural survival in a multiethnic diaspora. These are much bigger than my individual experiences of being called "kike," or having a schoolmate hiss at me that "Jews are going to hell for killing Christ." Similarly I have trouble relating to trans movements that focus on gender expression as some kind of self-actualization project, or academic pomo treatises on the de(con)struction of gender, rather than looking at gender liberation—which is not about the struggle to find the perfect term for our unique individual sense of self, the perfect packer, or even our struggles to access healthcare or fight employment discrimination: it's about Chinese women going blind at 25 because they've been soldering microscopic parts in a microchip factory for the last ten years, or Filipina women having to leave their families to look after white babies in North America. On a global level, struggles about gender are more about colonialism, capitalism, and racism than about individual identity. There is a lot of talk about the "interconnectedness of oppressions", but are we carrying that through to how we fight for justice as trans people? I don't see that broader understanding of gender oppression reflected in most of the writing and talking about trans issues. That's our failure to think of the interconnectedness when we think of what "trans issues" are.

At 20, I thought I knew all the answers. At 30, I know I don't have any answers. I don't know yet how to integrate my work as a trans activist with my work to support indigenous sovereignists, end the violence of the Israeli occupation as a necessary step to a lasting and just peace in the Middle East, or any of the bigger picture survival issues. I certainly don't know how to resolve the contradictions between believing in economic justice and participating daily in the brutality of capitalism. It is frustrating. But there is also something reassuring in knowing that many other people are wrestling with these same questions.

We're just about to celebrate Pesach (Passover), an annual celebration of ancient Jewish liberation from slavery that asks hard questions about commitment and collective responsibility. When I sit at my family's holiday seder table and clasp hands with people of all genders who have been fighting their whole lives for justice, hundreds of years collectively between us and thousands more in the ghosts around the table, I will think of the next decade not only as a struggle for my day-to-day survival, but for the survival of the entire world as we lurch ever on towards freedom.

ADDITIONAL RESOURCES

BIBLIOGRAPHY

FTM: Female-to-Male Transsexuals in Society
Holly Devor (Indiana University Press)

Becoming a Visible Man
Jamison Green (Vanderbilt University Press)

Body Alchemy: Photographs
Loren Cameron. (Cleis)

Gender Outlaw
Kate Bornstein (Vintage)

GenderQueer: Voices from Beyond the Sexual Binary
Joan Nestle et al. (Alyson)

The Phallus Palace
Dean Kotula (Alyson)

Transgender Care: Recommended Guidelines, Practical Information, and Personal Accounts
Gianna E. Israel et al. (Temple University Press)

Transgender Warriors
Leslie Feinberg (Beacon)

True Selves: Understanding Transsexualism
Mildred L. Brown et al. (Jossey-Bass)

ONLINE RESOURCES

FTM Organizations

Amboyz   www.amboyz.org/

Compass www.geocities.com/ftmcompass/
FTM Alliance of Los Angeles www.ftmalliance.org/

159

FTM Australia   torque.ftmaustralia.org/

FTM International   www.ftmi.org/

FTM London   www.ftmlondon.org.uk/

FTM Support of Kansas City   kansascityftms.bravepages.com/

Tarheel Transmen (North Carolina)   www.geocities.com/
tarheeltransmen/

GENDERQUEER RESOURCES

www.genderesistant.org

www.genderblur.org/

PERSONAL WEBSITES

www.transgenderwarrior.org (Leslie Feinberg's website)

www.jamesgreen.com/   (long-time director of FTM Int'l)

www.otherbear.com/home.html   (Michael Hernandez's website)

GENERAL INFO WEBSITES

www.gender.org/resources/female_to_male.html

www.ftm-intl.org

www.ftminfo.net/   FTM Informational Network

www.thetransitionalmale.com/

www.ftm.org.uk/

About the Authors

Gavriel Alejandro Levi Ansara is a polycultural, polyglot, gay Jewish FTM with ties to China, Australia, and several other locales. His deepest pleasures in life are paradigm-shifting conversations, weightlifting, opera, theatre, culinary creations, literature, performance art, social justice, community service, and so many other marvelous pursuits that a complete list would make your mind reel.

Cooper Lee Bombardier hails from Abington, MA, but has recently moved to New Mexico. Cooper Lee has been a featured artist in The National Queer Arts Festival as well as the groundbreaking Trans/Art 2001 show. Cooper was part of the first Sister Spit Tour in 1997 and appears on both of the Sister Spit CDs. Cooper has appeared on book covers such as *The Drag King Book* and has also starred in several independent films, including *The Ride* by Bill Basquin. Cooper has taught art and creative writing to young people in San Francisco through WritersCorp, but currently pays the bills as a union builder.

Ali Cannon, a Jewish FTM, is a writer of short stories, poetry and theatre pieces. His illumination of Jewish and transgender themes can be seen in the film, *It's A Boy: Journeys from Female to Male* and his published essay (co-authored with TJ Michels) *"Whose Side Are You On? Transgender at the Western Wall"* (*Queer Jews,* Routledge). He has been writing and performing original works extensively in the San Francisco Bay Area, performing with a range of theatre collectives including *Chutzpah, Transmen Tell Their Tales, Everyday People, and Ego Alter Ego.* He has appeared on stage at Luna Sea, Theater Rhinoceros, the LGBT Center in SF, the True Spirit Conference, and most recently in Sacramento as part of the Lambda Players season. He is working on a full-length play, entitled *On Whales, War and Bad Men.* For strength and sustenance he thanks his wife, Jessica.

Rabblerouser and writer **Eli Clare** lives in Vermont and is the author of *Exile and Pride: Disability, Queerness, and Liberation* (South End Press, 1999).

Rian Fierros is a Spanish, Irish, and German writer living in San Francisco and is a contractor for Wells Fargo Bank. He has transitioned while on the job with no problems. He is completely out to family and friends, as well as his co-workers. He recently finished writing his first feature length screenplay, an FTM love story.

Storm Florez is a fire walking, folk rockin' love activist, and sensitive new age guy from Berkeley, CA. S/he is devoted to finding ways to UNidentify himself and others through building and tearing down personal structures and beliefs. Storm is a foolish devotee of LOVE whose main goal in life is to serve LOVE on a silver platter and spread it like butter across the path to personal freedom. You can find Storm performing around the Bay Area as a solo folk rock artist. Currently, Storm teaches classes in Toltec Shamanism to genderqueers of all persuasions.

Joshua Mira Goldberg is a big fish in a little pond. Growing up with sayings *like "Az di bobe volt gehat beytsim volt zi geven mayn zeyde"* (If my grandmother had testicles she would be my grandfather), he thinks it is small wonder he turned out to be a *faygele boychik*. Born in Vancouver, he and his Jewntile huzbear recently moved back to the big city after a 15-year dry spell without perverse Yiddish humor. He is glad to be home.

Cj Gross is a Special Education teacher and clown living in San Francisco CA for 13 years. Cj's interests include gender politics, gardening, spirit, sexual magic, and practicing the art of being fully alive.

Imani Henry is an activist, writer and performer. He is a contributor to the newly released IAC publication, *War in Colombia: Made in the USA*. Since 2002, he has toured nationally with his multimedia theatre piece, *B4T (before testosterone)*, which explores race, sexuality and gender expression through the lives of three Black, masculine female-bodied people. Currently, Imani, is developing his new work "The Strong Go Crazy: The Series" as an Artist in Residence at the Brooklyn Arts Exchange. *If I Should Die Before I Wake, Don't Let Me* is dedicated in loving memory of African-American Trans activist Alexander John "Bear" Goodrum.

Michael "Mike" Hernandez is a queer transbear, an author and public speaker who just happens to pay the bills through the practice of law. Mike has been of service to the transmen's community via his work with FTM Alliance of Los Angeles, Inc. (www.ftmalliance.org), and as one of the organizers of the 1999's

Forward Motion Conference. Writing credits include "The Art of Cruising Men" in *FORGE*, a sex column in the *FTMI Newsletter* (www.otherbear.com), and works in *Bears on Bears* (Alyson), *Transliberation: Beyond Pink And Blue* (Beacon), *Dagger: On Butch Women* (Cleis), and *The Second Coming*.

Mykkah Herner is a queer (gender, sexuality, and sex) writer. He generally writes snappy, sexy, smutty snips about bodies interacting, play(fullness), sex, queerness, gender, his two very loud and needy cats, or some combination thereof.

David Husted is a 38-year-old, FTM, divorced parent of one, who makes his home on the Central Coast of California. Living a mostly reclusive and private live, he fills his time with family and the arts.

Martin Inane is the pseudonym of Martin Macor, who is currently pursuing graduate studies in the American novel and queer theory. His photography has been exhibited at San Francisco's Balazo Gallery; as a model, he has sat for photographers Loren Cameron, Barbara DeGenevieve, and Larry Utley. "Punk Rock Carnival Whores" is dedicated to the memory of Daddy Alan Selby, friend and founder of Mr. S Leather.

Jordy Jones is an artist, writer, curator and community advocate. He has worked artistically with venues as diverse as San Francisco's Queer Cultural Center, NYC's Guggenheim Museum, and the De Waag Society for Old and New Media in Amsterdam. He is proud to serve on the LGBT Advisory Committee of the San Francisco Human Rights Commission and the Board of Directors of the San Francisco LGBT Pride Celebration Committee. He is past co-chair of the San Francisco Transgender Civil Rights

Implementation Task Force. He is pursuing a Master's degree in Museum Studies at SFSU.

Matt Kailey is a 47-year-old gay transman living in Colorado. His non-fiction has appeared in *San Francisco Frontiers*, *Out Front Colorado*, and *Equal Times Colorado*. His fiction has appeared in *Best Transgender Erotica* (Circlet Press) and in *Transgender Tapestry*. Matt writes a regular column for the Gender Identity Center of the Colorado Journal.

Rocco Rinaldi Kayiatos, the artist known as Katastrophe, has performed spoken word across the country with Sister Spit's Ramblin Roadshow, and the Wasted Motel Tour. He was a feature of the documentary film *Poetic License*, about youth poetry slams. His band, The End of the World, was recently nominated for an AVN Award, but unfortunately lost to Snoop Dogg. He's giving the trans community a voice in hip hop.

Juan Lamas-Iocco is a working class Latino/Hispanic Transgendered Butch who currently resides in Sydney, Australia. Auto mechanic by day and closet writer by night, he is a published writer and playwright currently working on a half-hour network television drama. Also the founder of Queer Latinos, for those born with female bodies who ID transsexual, transgender, intersex, queerly-gendered, third gender, stone/butch.

Tucker Lieberman is a 22-year-old novelist who likes sunflower seeds, the city of Providence, Rhode Island, and world peace. He transitioned in high school and graduated in 2002 from Brown University where he majored in Philosophy. *RFD*, *White Crane Journal*, *FTM International*, and *Transgender Tapestry* have published his words, and he has read at the University of Rhode Island and

Princeton University. His personal essays on transsexuality can be found in *Finding the Real Me: True Tales of Sex & Gender Diversity* (Jossey-Bass), and *Becoming: Young Words on Gender, Sexuality, and Identity*. *The Insatiable Adventures of the Eunuch Monks of Krat* is his first novel.

Mac McCord is an FTM living in the Blue Ridge Mountains of Northern Virginia. He is a published author and artist who plays bagpipes and pennywhistle with several Celtic bands in the area. He is a dog trainer by trade and has a Basset Hound Rescue kennel. He has a thing for mountain biking and dragons.

blake nemec is a working class sex worker, HIV counselor, writer, and brass band/ gay rap/ electro musician who lives in San Francisco. Ze has been active with media and self-sufficiency skillshare projects throughout the US, and currently works to create better health and equal rights for trans, homeless, sex worker, and HIV at risk or positive people as initial steps towards building self sufficient, non-capitalist infrastructures.

Boots Potential is a transboygirl fagdyke living in Seattle, where monster engages in low-level acts of hooliganism. He is a B-movie monster-gendered, bicycle-riding fiend who spraypaints for fun and for liberation. Monster is a science nerd and co-facilitates a political reading brigade.

Sailor Raven is a genderqueer youth/chicken type. Ze currently resides in Oakland, California, a transplant from the lovely midwest. Ze is involved in various grassroots organizing and educational projects. Ze has two zines: *body/WORDS* (which contains the piece winter/transition) and *Monsters In My House* – a new zine about family, race, growing up and lots of other stuff. Ze is a sex educator and veggie-eating sillypants on the side.

Johnny Giovanni Righini is a 21-year-old gender expressionist living in San Francisco. Transgender education and activism are two of his passions. He loves to express himself through photography art, and stomp on society's stereotypes in his highest pair of hot pink stilettos.

Westley Rutter is a pre-op, pre-t FTM transsexual who is queer identified. Some of his interests include queer studies, radical activism, art type stuff, and looking tough but being sweet.

Patrick Skater lives in Tucson, Arizona. He and his partner of 11 years have three grown sons. He is a social worker working within the Harm Reduction, Recovery Model. Patrick has used writing as a form of healing and advocates this process both in his personal and professional life to others who are searching for their own truths.

Captain Snowdon is a poet, street outreach worker, and the founder of the Queer Words Project in Victoria, BC. Captain is the author of two chapbooks: *Offending Intimacies* and *The Energy of Wordless Space*. Captain's videopoems have been screened at the Vancouver Videopoem Festival and the Seattle Poetry Festival. Captain is currently working on an experimental fiction piece entitled "Missing Boi" and continues to co-edit the transqueer zine *Avoid Strange Men*.

Daniel Soltis is a medical writer and freelance illustrator living in the San Francisco Bay Area. He documented much of his transition in comics, illustrations and essays, many of which have ended up on his webpage (www.coyotecomics.com) or in zines.

Dean Spade is a radical lawyer residing in New York City. He is the founder of a poverty law project that focuses on the needs of low-income trans and gender variant New Yorkers. He is also the co-editor of *makezine.org*.

Wyatt Swindler is a twenty-year-old black trannyfag currently residing in Minneapolis, MN. He fancies himself a writer, and photographer. Wyatt is looking forward to becoming a teacher, general contractor and a star drag queen and king.

Marcus Rene Van is a performance poet. He uses poetry to fuse realistic tales about being a Transgendered poet of color with his love of hip-hop. He has traveled to venues all over the nine counties of the Bay Area and beyond, spitting bold lyrics to incense racist and homophobic minds.

Reid Vanderburgh, MA, is a transman and psychotherapist in Portland, Oregon. Reid began his transition when he was 40 years old, after spending an unconscious, unhappy 22 years in the lesbian community. He's a lot happier now! Visit Reid on the web at www.transtherapist.com.

Eli Wadley lives in San Francisco and is a gardener by day and a social justice activist by night. He would like to thank everyone who played a part in his life, making him what he is today.